Praise for

"In his newest must-read book, *So, What's Your Proposal? Shifting High-Conflict People from Blaming to Problem-Solving in 30 Seconds*, Master Attorney/Mediator/ Therapist, Bill Eddy shows you how to stop the blame game and consciously shift conflict quickly into creative solutions. This book is crucial for anyone who has to deal with difficult people at home or in business!"
—Mari J. Frank, Esq. CIPP, attorney/mediator, and author of *Negotiation Breakthroughs*; co-author of *The Gift in Conflict for Couples*

"Not only does Bill's book show "how to" redirect judgmental dialogue to problem-solving focus, he, also explains why this simple 3-step process works. All the reader has to do is practice, practice, practice. What a wonderful resource in dealing with persons unable to focus on solving the problem."
—Sheldon (Shelly) E. Finman, Family Law Attorney & Mediator, Ft. Myers, Florida

"In *So, What's Your Proposal?* Bill Eddy explores the neuropsychology of high conflict personalities (HCPs) and furnishes a useful chart of left and right brain responses as a prelude to examining possible professional responses to such individuals. He then gives examples of ways to manage HCPs in a variety of situations, including mediation, work, education, families, communities, volunteer and non-profit organizations, and in politics. For someone who is not already familiar with Bill's analysis, this book provides some practical ways for professionals to deal with this frustrating class of clients. If you already know Bill's work, this book will still provide you with some new insights."
—Lawrence D. Gaughan, J.D., LL.M. Professional Director, Family Mediation of Greater Washington

"This is nothing short of brilliant. I spend a lot of time negotiating settlements in contentious divorce cases. This process is revolutionary in helping people moving through difficult negotiations. I wish I had this years ago."
—Molly B. Kenny, Attorney, Seattle, Washington

"*So, What's Your Proposal?* is a question literally designed to short-circuit the brain in stressful situations. Using the techniques described by attorney Bill Eddy in this work, you can immediately stop the negativity and gently shift participants from all-or-nothing into flexible thinking. This practice is useful not just for those of us who deal with high conflict people, but in any situation where the parties are stuck in negotiations and need to generate creative options."
—Michèle Huff, J.D., lawyer/meditator and author of *The Transformative Negotiator: Changing the Way We Come to Agreement from the Inside Out*

SO, WHAT'S YOUR PROPOSAL?

Shifting High-Conflict People
from Blaming to Problem-Solving
in 30 Seconds!

Bill Eddy, LCSW, Esq.

Attorney, Mediator and Therapist

UNHOOKED BOOKS
an imprint of High Conflict Institute Press
Scottsdale, Arizona

Copyright © 2014 by Bill Eddy
Unhooked Books, LLC
7701 E. Indian School Rd., Ste. F
Scottsdale, AZ 85251
www.unhookedbooks.com

ISBN: 978-1-936268-62-7
eISBN: 978-1-936268-63-4

Library of Congress Cataloging-in-Publication Data
Eddy, William A.
   So, what's your proposal? : shifting high-conflict people from blaming to problem-solving in 30 seconds! / Bill Eddy.
      157 pages cm
      ISBN 978-1-936268-62-7 (paperback)
   1. Interpersonal conflict. 2. Interpersonal relations. 3. Conflict management. I. Title.
BF637.I48E33 2014
153.4'3--dc23
2014022679

Cover design by Gordan Blazevik
Interior design by Jeff Fuller, Shelfish.weebly.com
Edited by Catherine Broberg

Printed in the United States of America

Also by Bill Eddy

It's All Your Fault at Work!
Managing Narcissists and Other High-Conflict People

BIFF: Quick Responses to High-Conflict People, Their Personal
Attacks, Hostile Email, and Social Media Meltdowns
Second Edition

It's All Your Fault!
12 Tips for Managing People Who Blame Others for Everything

High Conflict People in Legal Disputes

New Ways for Work Coaching Manual & Workbook:
Personal Skills for Productive Relationships

Don't Alienate the Kids!
Raising Resilient Children While Avoiding High Conflict Divorce

Splitting: Protecting Yourself While Divorcing Someone with
Borderline or Narcissistic Personality Disorder

Managing High Conflict People in Court
　　New Ways for Families in Separation and Divorce:
　　Professional Guidebook
　　Parent Workbook
　　Collaborative Parent Workbook
　　Decision Skills Class Instructor's Manual & Workbook
　　Pre-Mediation Coaching Manual & Workbook

Acknowledgements

I am very appreciative of my wife, Alice, for coping with yet another book! Her patience, personality, knowledge, critical feedback and overall positive spirit have helped me in uncountable ways. I am very thankful for the positive feedback and flexible-but-structured approach that Megan Hunter has provided me in guiding this book to publication, as well as testing its principles in her own work. I want to thank the following professional colleagues for giving me specific feedback on this method or the text: Michael Lomax, Sheldon Finman, Leonard Szymczak, Mari Frank, Molly Kenny, Larry Gaughan, Stephen Gambescia, Bonnie Elias, Teresa Brook, and John Edwards. Over the years, many friends have helped me think through the concepts described in this book and others, including Dennis Doyle, Austin Manghan, Norma Mark and uncountable others. I also appreciate the countless hours the High Conflict Institute team has contributed to developing and promoting our high-conflict work, including Michelle Jensen, Trissan Dicomes, Diane Buchman and Sue Taylor. I must acknowledge the many clients who have shown me how effective this method can be, as they successfully applied it to resolve disputes which were often quite complicated and heated – I have learned so much from you. Finally, I want to acknowledge the hard work of my editor, Catherine Broberg, who helped turn my conversational writing style into proper English without losing my conversational intent.

Contents

Introduction

Complain! Complain! Complain!

Blame! Blame! Blame!

Have you ever dealt with a high-conflict person—or anyone—who blames you or others for one problem after another, without taking any responsibility themselves? Don't you feel like just screaming at them?

Instead, consider using the simple methods taught in this book for getting them out of the past and away from blaming everyone else. Get them to quickly focus on the future, take responsibility, and contribute to finding solutions to problems—including those they created themselves.

When people complain and blame you, you don't need to defend yourself or respond with anger. Just calmly say: "So, what's your proposal?" and focus on teaching the simple three-step method explained in this book. This method will help you stay calm and confident, while earning the respect of those around you—even those who want to blame you!

And blame is abundant these days! Every day dozens—if not hundreds—of people confront us at work, at the store, in our communities, and online. Nerves get on edge. Look around; more and more people seem to blame others for anything that goes wrong in their lives. With high-conflict people increasing in society, with the 24-hour news cycle, and with Twitter, Facebook, and the Internet, we are constantly barraged with stories about the worst behavior of people and a plethora of terrible incidents every day. The strong temptation is to react and deflect blame back on them. However, this just feeds the problem.

This book lays out a simple, proven method to shift the conversation from the past and blame, to the future and problem solving. The method is extremely effective; we have seen it work over and over again—many times in just 30 seconds. What's more, almost anyone can use it—it just takes practice, and this book offer lots of examples to help you get started.

About My Background

I am a mediator, a lawyer, and a therapist. Over 30 years ago, I began counseling children and families in psychiatric hospitals and outpatient clinics. At the same time, I started volunteering as a community mediator and became attracted to resolving all types of disputes: neighbor disputes, business disputes, family disputes, etc. Then, 20 years ago, I went to law school and became a full-time lawyer and mediator, primarily of family disputes.

By putting together my experience from these three fields (therapy, mediation, and law), and through reading a lot of research, I realized that people with difficult personalities were becoming more common in society and that they liked to go to court—but rarely accepted the decisions made in court. So they went back over and over again, and developed reputations as "high-conflict" individuals.

With my background as a therapist and experience with mediation, I started learning about how to manage high-conflict legal cases in new ways. I became fascinated with developing simple methods to help ordinary people manage "high-conflict" people in all kinds of settings. First, I taught these methods to legal and workplace professionals (lawyers, judges, mediators, counselors, human resource professionals, and others). Now I am writing books and making videos for anyone who is interested in learning these simple methods and reducing the conflict in their own lives.

One of the most amazing discoveries has been the "So, what's your proposal?" method. It is both highly effective and easy to use. With practice and repetition, almost anyone can learn it. That's why I wrote this book—to teach the method to readers and to offer them examples and ideas for implementing this tool in their own lives.

About This Book

This book is purposefully short and simple. "So, what's your proposal?" is a very easy question to ask, so we won't spend a lot of time talking about the exact wording to use. Rather, we'll focus on the specifics to help you make the most of this question, including the language to use, when to ask it, what to watch out for, and how to solve problems after the other person or people start thinking about proposals. The first four chapters focus on explaining the basics of asking for proposals, teaching anyone how to make good proposals, and understanding high-conflict people. The rest of the book provides lots of examples of using this technique in different settings, inspired by real situations although most names and facts have been changed.

Each chapter also includes additional tips about solving problems and negotiating with high-conflict people and others. This includes information about brainstorming, making choices, and explaining the consequences of various proposals and choices. These principles can be useful in any setting, beyond the chapters in which they appear. The simple focus of this book is quickly shifting people—especially high-conflict people—from blaming and *all-or-nothing thinking* into *flexible thinking*, which is where most modern problems get solved.

I hope you find this helpful in dealing with the high-conflict people in your life—or anyone!

CHAPTER ONE

Will Emma and Jake Ever Agree?

"So, what's your proposal?" I asked Emma. She was complaining about her husband, Jake, whom she was divorcing. I was their divorce mediator. I could see Jake simmering on the other side of my round mediation table. I didn't know when he would start yelling at her again.

"What do you mean?" she asked, irritated at my interruption.

Jake wanted a 50-50 co-parenting schedule and she had been criticizing his parenting skills.

"You don't know anything about their schoolwork! You've never attended a parent-teacher conference! You work late all the time!" she said, then proceeded to go on and on about all of his weaknesses as a parent. Were they true? Or not? That wasn't for me to decide.

I learned a long time ago that telling someone like Emma to stop criticizing her husband or to stop talking about the past would just trigger more defensiveness. She would think that I was taking Jake's side and I'm supposed to be neutral as a mediator. So, without criticizing her at all, I just asked: "So, what's your proposal?" in an effort to shift her from blaming to problem solving.

The situation was tense. I also knew that Jake was about to angrily defend himself. People in his shoes in a divorce mediation typically—and angrily—say something like: "That's not true! I know a lot about their homework! I attended a parent-teacher conference a year or two ago! I don't come home from work late every night—I can change my schedule for the nights I have the children!"

And I knew that after he defended himself, she would

predictably defend her position, saying, "Tell me one thing about what C.J. and Mac are learning at school this week! Yeah, you attended a parent-teacher conference *once* in five years! If you could change your schedule so easily, why didn't you do it when we lived together and I was taking care of the kids 90 percent of the time!"

Letting Emma criticize Jake or letting him defend himself would be an endless cycle—and it will not bring them any closer to resolving their conflict.

"What I mean," I said, "is that it's best to make a proposal whenever you have a concern or criticism of the other parent. Remember, when we started the mediation, I said that we would be focusing on the future and what you want rather than rehashing the past and what you don't want. So, how would you turn your concerns into a proposal?"

"Oh, that's right. I forgot," Emma said with a frown, but she quickly calmed down and sat up in her seat. "I suppose that my proposal would be that Jake have the children every other weekend and that I have them during the week."

"No way!" exclaimed Jake. "I want 50-50 and that's all there is to it!" Then he turned to me and insisted, "I need to defend myself here after everything she's said!"

You Don't Have to Defend Yourself

"Actually, you don't have to defend yourself here at all—not in mediation," I quickly replied. "I'm just a neutral person and I don't pay much attention to what each of you says about the past and each other's behavior. Remember, I'm not a judge of the past. My focus is on the future and helping you reach agreements about how to manage it as parents. Now Emma has made a proposal. Do you remember our method for responding to that?"

"I forget. Can you remind me?" Jake answered, as he eyed Emma and took a deep breath.

"First," I said, "you can ask her questions about her proposal—

like when the weekend would start and end. Some people start weekends Saturday morning and end Sunday night. Others start the weekend Thursday evening—in which case you would take them to school on Friday—and end Monday morning by delivering them to school. So it's very common to ask, 'What do you mean in specific terms?' when she says you could have every other weekend.

"Then," I continued, "after you've gotten answers to all of your questions, just say, 'Yes, I can agree to that,' 'No, I'm not willing to do that,' or 'I'll think about it.' That's all you have to say."

"Well, I certainly don't agree with her having almost 90 percent of the parenting time," he said. "She wants too much control over the children. She doesn't really want me to spend any time with them!"

"That's not true," Emma said quietly, shaking her head no.

"Jake, let's not get ahead of ourselves. First, did you have any questions for Emma about her proposal?" I replied, trying to ignore their fast complaints about each other. I wanted to keep them focused on this very simple three-step process of making proposals, asking questions, and giving a short response.

"No!" he said emphatically. "But wait. What *did* you mean by every other weekend? When would I get the kids and when would you get them back—in your propoooooosal?" He dragged out the word.

"I resent that tone of voice!" Emma exclaimed. "Bill, tell him not to talk to me that way."

"Actually, I want to remind both of you that we'll have a better shot at reaching a workable agreement if you can avoid commenting on each other in any way—and commenting on each other's comments, if you know what I mean. Can you both agree to try that?"

They both nodded their heads yes. I knew they wanted to reach agreements and move forward in their lives. They weren't just arguing for the sake of arguing. They were both sincere in their points of view—they were just anxious about being away from their children and in different ballparks about how to schedule time with them.

Ignore Most Comments

I continued: "You can mostly ignore comments, intentions, tone of voice, arguments about fairness, and other side issues by staying focused on the details of your proposals, asking questions, and then responding to the proposals. So Emma, go ahead and see if you can answer Jake's question about your proposal."

"Oh yeah," she replied. "Um . . . you could pick them up right when school gets out on Fridays and return them to me on Sundays at six in the evening."

"And that's only every other weekend?" Jake exclaimed. "I'd be nuts to accept *your* limitations on *my* time with our kids. And I'm not doing all the driving."

Stay focused, I told myself. *I know this can work.* I turned to Jake and asked: "So is that a yes, a no, or an I'll think about it?"

"Well, I would say 'Yes' to that schedule for the weekends. But I want more time during the week! I want to help them with their homework and put them to bed at night—more than just the weekend. I want 50-50!"

"So that's a 'Yes' on your weekend schedule!" I exclaimed. "Does that mean, Jake, that you agree to Emma's proposal of *alternate* weekends? I'm just speaking of the weekends for right now."

"Yes," Jake replied.

"I think that means you have an agreement," I exclaimed. "Is that correct, Emma? If so, I better write that down."

"That's a 'Yes,'" she agreed reluctantly. "But he's not good at helping the children with their homework, so I'm not agreeing to weekdays and I'm not agreeing to 50-50."

"Well, hold on," I said. "You have an agreement for the weekends. Let me write that down before we get into proposals about the weekdays."

They were silent as I wrote and spoke out loud: "Emma and Jake agree that each parent shall have the children on alternate weekends from Friday after school through Sunday at 6 p.m. Oh wait," I said. "Does that mean Dad picks up the children Friday afternoon at school or that they walk home to Dad's house?"

I wanted them to stay focused on details, so they wouldn't slip back into bickering.

"I'll pick them up," Jake said.

"Good!" Emma exclaimed. "They like it when he picks them up at school."

Stay Focused

"Did you hear that, Jake?" He nodded. "It's always helpful to recognize the good things that each other does—both ways.

"Now," I said. "Jake, I think you were about to make a proposal. What were you going to say a couple minutes ago?"

"I want at least one weekday overnight, but I'd really like two. I don't see why I shouldn't just have 50 percent of the parenting time. I know that's what I'd get at court. In fact, this is ridiculous. I just—"

"Hold on," I interrupted. "Let's stay focused on what you want in here right now. Save your discussion of court for the end of the mediation session—if you haven't reached enough agreements. Right now, let's focus on your proposal."

"I can tell you right now that I don't agree," Emma said.

"Hang on," I interrupted Emma. "First, do you have any questions for Jake?"

By slowing down the fast responses, I can get them to think about details, which tends to help them stay calm and rational and focused on problem solving, rather than angry and extreme in their thinking.

"No," she responded. "I've always been the primary parent and Jake always gets home late from work."

"I can get home early on the nights I have the kids," Jake

said with frustration. "I told you, my boss said I can change my schedule one or two days a week."

"Well," Emma replied. "If you're getting off when school gets out on Fridays, that's one day right there. So you could only have one more day a week when you have weekends." Emma smiled like she had scored a small victory.

"I can get off more nights during the week—I know my boss will let me. Give me a break, can't you?" Jake's frustration was wearing thin. "I really think I should just go to court, Bill. She's trying to prevent me from seeing my kids."

Will He Walk Out?

He's about to walk out, I said to myself. Sometimes that happens, although they usually come back when I say we're just taking a break. What can I do? Oh that's right, I can make a proposal.

"You know, I propose that we take a few minutes for me to meet with each of you separately. Do you want to try that?"

"That's okay with me," Emma said.

"And me," Jake replied, exasperated. "I just want more time with my kids."

"Who wants to go first?" I asked.

They looked at each other. "Why don't you meet with him first, Jake?" Emma finally said. "You look pretty frustrated. And you're talking about court, which I think would be a big mistake."

I looked at Jake. "Okay," he said.

"Emma," I said as she got up, "feel free to sit in the lobby or walk around. I'll come and get you in 5 to 10 minutes for your turn. And by the way, I don't try to make these turns exactly the same minutes, so there's no need to keep track."

After she left the room, Jake said to me, "You know, I think I can win this in court. I know a lot of dads who are getting 50-50 parenting schedules."

"You might be right," I said, "although most of the 50-50 schedules I know about are by agreement rather than ordered by the court. I have several of those cases coming out of my mediations—and they work pretty well, because those schedules are agreed to fairly quickly and easily. But most of my cases are not 50-50. The parents agree on something that fits their work schedules, their children's activity schedules, and their parenting history. So 50-50 isn't a slam dunk by any means."

"My lawyer told me that I should be able to get that."

"Again, you might be right; some people do get that schedule at court. But keep in mind that a 50-50 parenting schedule that's imposed by a judge will be resented by the parent who 'lost' and you need a high level of cooperation to manage a 50-50 schedule—what with all of the exchanges, keeping track of activity schedules, clothes, school trips, and so forth. It may be easier to have a working relationship if the two of you can make proposals that lead to an agreement here, in mediation."

"I suppose you're right. But if she won't let me have more than alternate weekends, I'm going to go to court."

"That's always up to you. Since you're already here, though, you might think of another proposal to make when we get back together after I meet with Emma. If you can be flexible, you may be able to come up with something that can become an agreement. You've heard what's important to her, so see if you can make a proposal that's a bridge between the proposals you have both said up to now. It can't hurt to try."

"Okay," Jake replied. "Should I tell her to come in now? I'll walk around for a few minutes—maybe I'll feel less frustrated."

It's All the Mediator's Fault!

When Emma sat down, she immediately said, "I don't think you're helping us very much. Are you sure you know what you're doing?"

After all of my work with this difficult couple, that statement was like a knife in my chest. I felt like screaming, "Who are you to be criticizing me? After all of the frustrations you—and your husband—have put me through!" But I was used to this. I often become the next "target of blame" when their favorite target is not around. So I reminded myself to stay calm and ask my favorite question:

"Well, what do you propose? You're already here and we have some time left. And you already reached an agreement on weekends. But it's up to you. What would you propose to do now?"

"I'm mostly worried about the kids," she replied. "I don't think they really like spending time with their dad. If they don't feel like it, I don't think they should have to go with him."

"I can understand your concerns. A lot of moms worry that dads are less experienced at raising the kids and don't really have enough time to spend with them—like getting home from work late and so forth. But it's also important to know that after a separation or divorce, a lot of fathers who weren't very involved before become really committed to raising their children and do a pretty good job. And there's research that says that fathers and mother contribute different qualities to the children's learning and that kids with uninvolved fathers are at a real disadvantage."

"Well, he can be involved on alternate weekends."

"I should also tell you that the courts and child development experts believe it's best for the children to have *significant* time with each parent. The child development people don't put a percentage on it and say doing so is a bad idea. But the courts like percentages and they are moving toward much more equal sharing of parenting time. It's possible that a judge could order you to have a 50-50 schedule—I'm starting to see that happen nowadays—or a schedule where you each have at least 35 percent of the time."

"Well, I'm not doing that—that's for sure," said Emma.

"You heard Jake say that he feels like going to court. If you want to avoid that, you might think of a proposal that he could agree to. Think about what you've heard him propose and see if you can come up with some kind of bridge proposal that could work for both of you. Otherwise, you may end up in court."

"Well . . . okay."

"Why don't you think about that while I go out and take a three-minute bathroom break and bring Jake back in."

"I guess so," Emma said, hesitantly.

Does Anyone Have a New Proposal?

When I got them back in the room together, I asked, "Does anyone have a new proposal?"

They looked at each other; then Jake said, "I'd like to have the children every Tuesday overnight, and Wednesdays I'd like to pick them up at school and take them to my office for a couple hours. Then, I'll bring them to your house. It's not exactly 50-50, but I can live with it."

Before Emma could respond (she was already shaking her head no), I asked her if she had any questions.

"How can you care for them at your office? That's a ridiculous idea. Why did you ever propose that?" she challenged.

I put up my hands, waving to both of them. "Hold on. Actually, let's avoid *Why* questions. They tend to start new arguments, because they're not really a question at all—they're a criticism of the proposal, and we don't need that. We just need your questions and then your responses: 'Yes,' 'No,' or 'I'll think about it.' Now I think you did have a *How* question—those are almost always good. Do you want to answer that, Jake?"

"You mean, how can I care for them at my office? I want them to see how I work. They can sit at chairs by my desk. I'll give them things to do—like drawing or playing games on their iPads."

"That's so absurd. You have no idea what you're talking about doing. They're six and eight years old!" Emma said.

"Hold on, Emma," I intervened. "Can you rephrase that as a question or a proposal?"

"You're right. I propose that you not have the children at your office every Wednesday after school. And I'll think about Tuesday's overnight. Would you pick them up at school? Is that what you're thinking?"

"Yes, I would get off early on Tuesdays and go home after I pick them up—or run errands. I won't go back to my office. Then I'll take them to school Wednesday morning."

"Umm . . . Okay, I'll do that—I'll agree to that. You can have them every Tuesday after school and return them to school Wednesday morning."

"So you're saying 'Yes' to that part of Jake's proposal?"

"Yes."

"Great! Let me write that down," I said. I said the agreement out loud as I wrote it down, as I did for the other agreements.

Then Jake added, "And I'll agree to withdraw my proposal for Wednesday afternoons at my office. I don't want to make it hard for the kids. As long as I have weekly Tuesday overnights."

"Thank you," said Emma.

"I'm not doing it for you. I'm doing it for the kids!" Jake exclaimed, angrily.

"Okay folks," I said. "It sounds like you have a full agreement on the weekly parenting schedule. There's no need to argue when you have an agreement. You made good proposals. You asked good questions. And now you have an agreement. Way to go!"

They both relaxed and looked relieved. Emma said, "We're making progress. We can do this."

Jake nodded in agreement. We weren't done with all of their issues—and all of their upsets—but we *were* making progress. They had started making agreements.

Comment

I wanted to start off with this common example, because everyone knows someone who's separating or getting a divorce. This story gives you an idea of how you can overcome blaming and defensiveness, in even the hardest of situations, by staying focused on asking "So, what's your proposal?" and dealing with resistance to solving problems—whether you're dealing with two people or just one person. While this is a simple question, you can see there are many distractions that come up, which I'll teach you how to deal with in the next few chapters.

In the next chapter, I'll explain why this approach really works—especially with high-conflict people, who are the most difficult people to focus on problem solving. Once you understand what I call the "Big Shift," it will get easier and easier to do this shift yourself, even when you're being intensely criticized or blamed at work, at home, or anywhere else.

CHAPTER TWO

The (Brain) Power of This Question

Emma and Jake in chapter 1 were highly stressed. They were making difficult decisions about sharing custody of their children after separating. But, with guidance, they were able to reach agreements! Could they have done this on their own? Very unlikely.

Why did the method of focusing on one simple question help them? How can you use this same method in everyday life to deal with difficult, or simply upset, people? This chapter explains why asking this question works so well and why it is so surprisingly simple, though not always easy.

Solving Conflicts under Stress

Brain research shows that we use two different types of thinking for responding to conflicts, one when we are relaxed and another when we are in a crisis. Different parts of the brain respond—automatically and instantly—depending on the circumstances.

Generally, our "problem-solving" brain is associated with the left hemisphere of our brains. Our "defensive reacting" brain is associated more with the right hemisphere. Of course, neuroscientists will tell you that these differences are not absolute and that there is a lot of overlap and interconnectedness between the two sides of our brains.

Since I'm not a brain scientist, I am just talking about general tendencies to guide your response with upset people, rather than trying to give you an anatomy lesson. Just think of this "right" brain and "left" brain point of view as an easy concept to remember when you're deciding how to respond to upset people.

Here's a chart showing some of the general differences in how we respond to conflict:

Two Different Ways We Solve Conflicts

LOGICAL PROBLEM SOLVING	DEFENSIVE REACTING
Focuses on analyzing problems	Focuses on fighting, fleeing, or freezing
Attacks the problem with curiosity	Attacks and blames the other person
Looks for a variety of good solutions	Sees only one desperate solution
Uses flexible thinking	Uses all-or-nothing thinking
Sees situation as an interesting problem	Sees situation as an extreme crisis
Feels need for a thorough analysis	Feels need for fast action to survive
Sees problems as complex	Sees problems as simple: bad people
Sees self as open to improvement	Sees self as blameless
Balances problems in context of other issues	Deals with problems out of context
Sees compromise as a normal part of life	Sees compromise as life threatening
Views fear and anger as manageable emotions that should not interfere with making good decisions	Views fear and anger as overwhelming emotions that call for quick, defensive action

Did you notice that these two approaches are almost opposite? When you're using one set of strategies, it's really hard to use the other strategies.

Crisis Shuts Down Logic (the Amygdala)

There's a part of our brains that shuts down our logical problem solving when we are in a crisis. It's called the amygdala ("uh-mig-da-la"). Each hemisphere of our brains includes an amygdala, which is generally responsible for how we react to signs of danger. The amygdala is fasting acting; it can shut down our logical problem solving in less than a hundredth of a second— before you're even conscious that you have switched to defensive reacting. Your feet may be running, your heart may be pumping, your voice may be yelling—all before you even realize you're doing anything.

This defensive reacting may save your life if you are facing a flood, a fire, a violent person, or some other crisis. That's the good news. The amygdala, especially the right amygdala, can set off a whole chain reaction of responses inside us: our hearts beat faster, shots of adrenaline and cortisol instantly pump through our bodies, muscles tighten, our visual focus narrows, and so forth.

The bad news is that most of the situations we encounter call for calm and logical problem solving, so that intense and dramatic defensive reacting can get us into trouble. Or it might trigger someone else's defensive reacting, so they want to fight us in order to feel safe themselves.

Overriding the Crisis Response

Scientists now contend that we can train ourselves to override our amygdala responses. The prefrontal cortex of the brain is the control center and it communicates directly with each amygdala, as well as many other parts of the brain. The prefrontal cortex can learn to tell the amygdala, "No, it's not a crisis," and thus stop or prevent the whole chain of fight-flight-freeze responses described above. But this training requires practice.

On its own, the right amygdala automatically, instantly, and unconsciously reacts defensively to facial expressions of fear and anger, to a negative tone of voice, and to hand gestures that appear threatening. (The left amygdala responds more to written words that seem threatening.) Again, this amygdala crisis response can occur in as little as six thousandths of a second—much faster than conscious thinking.

This built-in response also helps explain why children react defensively to threatening facial expressions, tones of voice, and other behaviors before they have even learned which are safe and which are not. A lot of adolescent development is about learning which situations are real crises or emergencies and which can be ignored or even enjoyed. Brain scientists now say that the adolescent brain is not fully developed until about age twenty-five.

But, again, with practice and preparation, we can automatically divert an amygdala crisis response before it gets started and instead stay calm and focused on problem solving.

If a crisis response does get triggered, we can still use methods to calm ourselves. As soon as we realize we are getting unnecessarily upset, for example, we can tell ourselves encouraging statements that will calm us down (see below). This is especially important when people around us are starting to get upset in response to each other—or to us!

Defensive Reacting Is Contagious

Since everyone else also has an amygdala in each hemisphere of their brain, when we're upset, they may easily respond by getting upset too. Indeed, brain scientists say that "emotions are contagious." As soon as one person starts *defensive reacting*, others nearby may start defensive reacting too. You can see this happening in families, with friends, at sporting events, in Internet chat groups, and lots of other settings. Once one person gets real upset, someone else usually does as well. The response seems to spread until everyone stops arguing or someone walks out of the whole situation.

But logical problem solving is also contagious. If the person in charge of a group or situation, or any important member of a group, can somehow convince the whole group to stay calm and logical, then it is possible that the upset emotions will dissipate and problem solving can occur. However, this depends on how many people are defensive reacting and how intense (and loud) they have become. If they are too upset, they may not be able to shift over to problem solving for a long time—like 20–30 minutes or sometimes several days. Once you are defending yourself, it takes a while to physically calm down and become logical again. It takes some time just for the adrenaline and cortisol—key fight-or-flight hormones—to exit our bloodstreams.

Mirror Neurons

Why is logical problem solving contagious? As we explained, the amygdala focuses on danger, not logic, so the contagious nature of logical problem solving involves another part of the brain called mirror neurons. Identified over the past fifteen years, these neurons seem to make us copy, or mirror, the behavior of those around us. If we're watching a ball game, for example, then in our own minds we are playing that ball game.

Mirror neurons may actually explain how children learn. They may also be the basis for empathy—which develops when we take on or actually *feel* what those around us are feeling. The closer your relationship with someone, the more you may experience the same joy and sadness that the other person feels.

You are also likely to "catch" the behavior of those around you and copy it. Likewise, the people near you are likely to catch your behavior. Like defensive reacting, however, you can override this effect once you are aware of it. This is important to understand if you want to influence the behavior of others and override their influence over you.

Corpus Callosum

Another part of the brain that also seems to affect our responses to problems is the corpus callosum—the thick "bridge" between the right and left brains that contains millions of neurons. This is the super highway where information flows between our brain hemispheres. It helps us use our left-brain problem-solving abilities and our right-brain creativity and self-protection abilities at the same time. However, one side seems to dominate the other at any given time. If we feel threatened enough, the right-brain defensiveness shuts off the left-brain problem solving and goes into fight, flight, or freeze mode—mostly driven by the right amygdala.

Unfortunately, some people have a smaller corpus callosum than others, which makes it harder for them to shift back to logical problem solving in their left hemisphere and instead remain upset and defensive in their right hemisphere. The reduced size of the corpus callosum may be connected to developmental problems that occurred before birth, such as genetic disorders or fetal alcohol syndrome, caused by the mother drinking while pregnant. Or the growth of the corpus callosum may be compromised in early childhood by child abuse, which triggers too much of the stress hormone cortisol in the child's brain, so that the neurons in the corpus callosum are blocked from getting enough sucrose, their usual source of nourishment.

And some people simply grew up without much practice at solving problems when they were upset—someone else did it for them. This, too, leads to fewer neural connections across the corpus callosum. As neuroscientists explain it, connections grow between neurons when two experiences occur at the same time, such as being upset (using the right brain) and finding solutions (using the left brain). "Neurons that fire together, wire together" is one of their common sayings.

Whatever the cause, the corpus callosum seems to be smaller

in some adults with personality disorders. Again, many grew up in abusive homes and were overwhelmed, so they didn't get help learning how to manage their own emotional upsets. Others grew up feeling entitled to and receiving everything they wanted, so they didn't learn how to manage themselves when they were upset. Since neurons grow connections from repeated use, this may explain why some people with personality disorders have a harder time shifting from defensive reacting back to logical problem solving. This is a common characteristic of people who seem to get stuck in conflicts and make them bigger, rather than reducing or resolving them.

High-Conflict People (HCPs)

Some people repeatedly get stuck in defensive reacting and have a hard time calming down and engaging in problem solving. I think of them as high-conflict people or HCPs (for references to the singular person who is high conflict, I'll use the abbreviation HCP). This behavior is a part of who they are—usually part of their personalities since they were children. They automatically get stuck in conflict and take it to a higher level and stay there (blaming others and not looking at themselves), rather than calming themselves and focusing on solutions. This is because they have four basic characteristics:

- Preoccupation with blaming others
- All-or-nothing thinking
- Unmanaged emotions
- Extreme behaviors

They become preoccupied with blaming others, arguing for just one solution, and doing all of the other things listed in the right-hand column of the above conflict chart, for months or years in some cases (especially if their behavior results in legal action). For more on HCPs, see my book *It's All Your Fault! 12 Tips for Managing People Who Blame Others for Everything.*

Why are some people like this? It may be the result of having a smaller corpus callosum, or from simply mirroring the behavior of those around them when they grew up—including too many extreme images on TV, movies, video games, and the Internet.

When high-conflict behavior becomes an automatic and unconscious pattern, individuals may become HCPs and repeatedly overreact to conflicts. In some ways, they are like alcoholics and addicts—they are in denial about their own problems and the situation may worsen if others try to persuade them to look at themselves.

However, it's not necessary to figure out whether someone is an HCP or to convince them anything about their behavior in order to help them shift out of its pattern. The simple three-step proposal method taught in the next chapter can be used with anyone at any time during a conflict. But it becomes more important to use this method if you are dealing with a high-conflict person, as many other tactics may unintentionally increase his or her high-conflict behavior and make the situation much harder on yourself.

The BIG SHIFT

In this book, we'll talk about making the "Big Shift." This refers to shifting yourself or someone else out of *defensive reacting* and into *logical problem solving*. When done correctly, this move can usually occur within 30 seconds. How do you trigger the shift? Begin by focusing on yourself. You can shift yourself with a brief encouraging statement or by asking one simple question of yourself: "So, what do you propose?" Yes, you can use this method on yourself!

Once you are familiar with this concept and have practiced asking yourself this question, you may begin using it almost automatically when you feel upset with someone else. Rather than reacting defensively, you can focus your thoughts on developing a proposal for managing the situation or resolving a conflict.

In brain terms, the shift moves you from defensive reacting

(right brain) to problem solving (left brain) by putting your feelings into words. Words seem to be primarily a left-brain function, so as soon as you identify your upset feelings with words, you tend to reduce the upset feeling (right) and become more logical (left).

For example, in his book *Blink*, Malcolm Gladwell explains that when a witness of a crime is asked what a suspect looks like, it is better for the witness to look at pictures or an artist's drawing (with suggestions for changes to make it more accurate) than to put his or her description into words. Just using words to describe the suspect interferes with the mental picture in the witness's mind and can distort it forever. Once again, this goes back to our right brains' focus on the visual and our left brains' focus on language. Whichever hemisphere is dominant at the time influences the perceptions of the other hemisphere. Put words to an upset feeling and the feeling changes and usually calms down.

High-conflict people are often overreacting and stuck in their right-brain defensiveness. If you tell them they are overreacting or tell them to "calm down," they will likely get angrier with you. This is because they are interpreting your tone of voice and facial expressions as threatening. Rather than shifting them, you are reinforcing their upset emotions by responding with your own *defensive reacting*.

Remember that you can override both the tendency to mirror other people's behavior and your amygdala response that is triggered by others' intense negative emotions. You don't have to react to them in kind. With this knowledge, you can avoid having a negative response like theirs and can instead *influence* their response in a positive direction.

So you can do something that will shift them into logical problem solving rather than increasing their defensive reacting. Something that focuses them on logic and problem solving. Something such as "So, what's your proposal?"

If you can do this with a positive tone of voice and an upbeat facial expression, they often will feel safe enough to automatically lower their defensiveness and actually think about what their proposal will be. But this doesn't work if you say it in a negative tone of voice or with a downbeat facial expression.

To be successful with this approach, you have to practice sincerely—truly, really, really wanting to know what the person's proposal is. Once you learn how to do this, you can effectively shift an upset person—including a constantly upset HCP—from blaming to problem solving in 30 seconds (or less!). It's a brain switch (apparently from right to left), and our brains can be very fast when we get the message right.

Shouldn't You Just Listen?

This approach may sound mechanical and insensitive. You may wonder whether this is the wrong way to deal with upset people: "Shouldn't you just let the person talk about their upset feelings to get them off their chest?" This is a good question and here is the answer: "It depends on the person and the situation." The average person can talk about their upset feelings with someone who cares and feel better pretty quickly. Sometimes just listening in a caring manner does help them resolve the issue for themselves.

However, one of the sad characteristics of high-conflict people is that they can talk and talk about their upset feelings without getting any relief. Even if they are talking to someone who cares deeply about them, listening alone will not serve them well—because they seem to lack the ability to heal and move forward in their lives. For them, talking about upset feelings may just reinforce being stuck in their right-brain defensiveness.

Whatever the reason—whether it's because of overwhelming childhood abuse, or a genetic tendency, or growing up entitled and always getting what they wanted—they seem unable to experience the normal human healing process of grieving and recovering and feeling better. Instead, they seem to go through life getting upset, then getting distracted from their upsets when they address or solve the problem at hand, which helps them feel better.

For this reason, HCPs are more preoccupied than the average person in talking about their problems—and especially about other people's past behavior toward them. Yet, talking about their feelings and the past for hours and hours does not bring them relief. What does often help is to *shift them away from their upset emotions* (after briefly acknowledging the emotions and showing empathy for them) and focus instead on tasks they can do now.

If you are individually dealing with such an upset person, you can give that person some good attention and then shift him or her over to problem solving by saying "How I can help you today is to focus on what you can do next. Here are some suggestions . . . So, which would you prefer to do now?" In a sense, you are acting as the person's corpus callosum—directing his or her attention away from upset emotions (right brain) and toward problem-solving activities (left brain). After you get used to doing this, you will be surprised at how frequently—and quickly—this produces positive results.

Shifting Two People at Once

If you are dealing with two people in a conflict, such as in the mediation in the first chapter, you may have to more quickly focus them away from their upset emotions and onto their proposals. That's why I don't ask for "opening statements" in a mediation when I suspect that the people involved may be high conflict. These statements tend to focus too much *on the past* and how bad they feel about it. Instead, I ask for their "initial thoughts and questions" regarding the decisions they need to make *about the future*. I explain that articulating these will help them make their proposals, which are at the center of the mediation process, so that they can eventually reach agreements. Otherwise, they get stuck in their defensiveness about the past and simply react to each other's comments, without focusing on the future and without finding a workable solution.

In other words, I don't expect that focusing on feelings will be at all productive with HCPs and so I quickly shift the focus to problem solving and try to keep it there. This often leads them to feeling better after all, because the problems they were upset about often get resolved for the future. It's like helping a child learn how to clean up spilled milk, rather than just letting him or her cry about it.

Therefore, it makes a difference whether you are dealing with an average person or a high-conflict person (perhaps 10–15 percent of the general population). The Big Shift is designed for HCPs, although it can help anyone when they are feeling stuck in upset emotions. It also makes a difference whether you are talking alone with an upset person, are managing two people in conflict, or are dealing with more people in a public situation. One-on-one, you can focus somewhat on feelings if that seems appropriate, but with HCPs it is most productive to emphasize future tasks since their emotions about the past often overwhelm them.

But when you are dealing with a conflict between two or more people directly and there is a lot of blaming going on, then the Big Shift may be a tool you'll need to use a lot. And one of the easiest ways to accomplish the Big Shift without triggering defensiveness is to simply and calmly ask "So, what's your proposal?"

Summary

In this chapter we have focused on why this question may be so powerful. Simply asking "So, what's your proposal?" may be successful because it can influence at least three aspects of the brain:

1. It helps calm the warning system associated with the brain's two amygdalae, especially the right amygdala, which may be larger for some people with high-conflict personalities.

2. It helps shift attention away from *defensive reacting* (a right-brain process) to *logical problem solving* (a left-brain process), which may really help people who are trapped in a defensive mode because of a smaller corpus callosum.

3. It may influence mirror neurons, so that they reflect your calmness and attention to problem solving.

Not only can you shift yourself, but you can accomplish the Big Shift for others—individually or together—by staying calm and managing your own emotions and behavior. You're not just shifting them from right-brain defensiveness to left-brain problem solving. You're also shifting responsibility for problem solving back onto their shoulders, if they may have tried to make you accountable for solving their problems. High-conflict people in general are preoccupied with blaming others and trying to hold others responsible for their own problems. By asking for *their proposals,* you are making it clear that you do not feel responsible for *solving their problems* but instead are willing to *assist them* in solving *their own problems.*

This takes practice. The next chapter will discuss ways to stay calm as you deal with a defensive person and help you learn how to teach upset people a simple three-step method for making proposals.

CHAPTER THREE

Making Proposals with Three Simple Steps

How can you accomplish the Big Shift by simply asking: "So, what's your proposal?" First, you need to learn ways of calming yourself—especially if you are the person being blamed. Then, you can teach them the three-step method.

Calming Yourself

One of the best ways to calm yourself is to offer yourself encouraging statements. Here are a few of my favorites for high-conflict situations:

It's not about me! It's about their difficulty managing themselves.

In other words, even if they're intensely blaming me, it's not really about you. It's about them and their lack of skills in managing their emotions and sharing responsibility for solving problems. Constructive feedback is never delivered in an angry, blaming manner. In fact, the more emotionally intense the blaming, the less likely it is to have anything constructive in it.

I don't have to defend myself. I'm doing fine as I am. They can't hear it now anyway.

When the other person is absorbed in anger and blaming, they are usually stuck in their right-brain defensive reacting. This means that logical information is out of reach for them at this time and explaining it would be a waste of energy. They just can't hear you in terms of useful information.

I don't have to feel what they are feeling. I can have my own feelings. Even if the person is not upset with you, he or she may try to get you to be upset with somebody else. You don't have to take on these same feelings. Instead, you can say that it sounds frustrating and then ask, "So, what do you propose?" This helps you stay out of the emotional part of the situation and can help you avoid pressure to take sides.

I'm not responsible for their problem. I can be supportive without getting too involved.

High-conflict people try to shift responsibility for their problems onto other people's shoulders. You don't have to be responsible for solving their problems, but you can be supportive—especially if the person is a friend, family member, co-worker, or neighbor whom you need to get along with. You can take the same approach to staying calm as in the preceding example: "That sounds like a difficult situation. What do you think you'll propose for solving it?"

Of course, another way of staying calm is to talk to a friend or someone else who is calm at the moment. Their calmness may be contagious and help you to feel better—even if you don't talk about the upsetting situation at all. That's up to you and the situation. Sometimes talking about being upset or stressed by someone else can make you feel better, and sometimes it can make you feel more upset. Another strategy to help you feel calmer is to just distract yourself, such as by going for a walk or listening to music.

Manage Your Tone of Voice

Now that you're calm, how should you speak to the upset person? You want to communicate your sense of calmness and one of the best ways to do this is to manage your own tone of voice—especially when you are speaking to a potentially high-conflict person. It also helps if you can sound truly interested in what the person has to say. If you sound mean, nasty, challenging, snarky, arrogant, insulting, as if you're looking for a fight, or not truly interested, then you will make things worse. Asking "So, what's your proposal?" is designed to calm the other person and help them focus on devising solutions to problems. If you say it as a challenge, then the person won't shift to problem solving but instead will stay defensive and likely increase their blaming.

Words You Can Use

You don't have to use the exact wording I've suggested in asking the question. You can ask:

*What would you **propose**?*
Sometimes this sounds softer than "proposals" and less threatening.

*What would you **suggest**?*
This is an easy alternative. You can only ask for "proposals" so many times.

*What are **some options** you would like me to consider?*
This is another alternative that shows you are interested and will consider what they say.

*Do you have **any ideas** that might solve this problem?*
Another easy alternative, this conveys the same interest and focus on solutions.

*I'm interested in **your thoughts** on what we should do here.*
By using the word "we" here, you show sincere interest in solving this together. It really gets away from shame and blame.

A Shift in 30 Seconds

The whole point is to lower the feeling of confrontation and to shift over to problem solving. Your tone and your words can accomplish that very quickly. I explained why it can work this way in chapter 2. Usually if this shift doesn't occur within 30 seconds, it is because your tone and words have hinted at confrontation, rejection, criticism, or negative judgment or that you have not explained how to make a proposal yet.

You can actually teach how to make a proposal very quickly, but you will need to repeat the instructions several times if the situation stays heated. Turn back to chapter 1 and notice how I repeated my explanation to Emma and Jake over and over again during the mediation. And eventually they did get it—at least while I kept focusing them on this question.

Explaining How to Make a Proposal

Any problem in the past can be turned into a proposal about the future. Proposals don't have to be complicated. You can just blurt one out during any conversation or while meeting with any group. Proposals get attention, because they offer solutions to past problems by focusing on the future.

Most of us are relieved to talk about the future, rather than what we've done wrong in the past. On the other hand, most of us easily slip into talking about the past or even get stuck talking about the past, including what everyone else has done wrong. The following explanation focuses on how to make proposals in a way that is easy and can be done at any time.

Three Simple Steps

Here are the three basic steps to making a proposal:

> ▶ **Step 1: Make a proposal.**
>
> ▶ **Step 2: Ask and answer questions about the proposal.**
>
> ▶ **Step 3: Respond with "Yes," "No," or "I'll think about it."**

Now, let's take a closer look at how you can use each step:

▶ **Step 1: Make a proposal.**
Ideally, proposals will include these elements: ***Who*** *does* ***What,*** ***When,*** *and* ***Where.***

For example: "I propose that you be the one who picks up Johnny after school and takes him to his soccer practice. Then, you can keep him overnight and bring him back to school the next morning."

This is much better than saying, "You never took Johnny to any of his soccer practices! You always left it up to me. Then you showed up on Saturday at his games and made it look like you were such an involved parent. I want some respect here for all I've done!" And then the other parent attacks back: "You never gave me a chance . . ." And on and on.

Can you see how it would have been so much simpler to just ask for what you wanted in the future by making a proposal? It avoids all of the blame and defensiveness that people get stuck in when they talk about the past.

So proposals are always about the future. They are not about the past or about the other person's intentions or *why* they made the proposal. *Why* questions easily turn into criticism.

"*Why* did you say that?" really means "I think that's a stupid idea and I want to force you to admit it." A better course of action, if you think the other person's proposal is a bad idea, is to just make another proposal and continue on this way until you can both agree on something.

▶ **Step 2: Ask and answer questions about the proposal.**
After one person has made a proposal, the other person may not be immediately sure whether it's agreeable or not. Therefore, it often helps to ask questions. One of the best questions here is "What would your proposal look like in action?" This helps you get clearer on the Who, What, Where, and When of the proposal. You might even ask, "What's your picture of how this would work?

What would you do? What would I do, if you could picture your proposal actually happening?"

Again, you don't want to ask *Why* questions, because that usually triggers defensiveness. And if someone becomes defensive, then it makes it hard for them to think of solutions. Watch out for challenging questions about a proposal, like "How do you expect me to do that?" "What were you thinking when you came up with that idea?" "Do you know that you never did that before?" or "Don't you realize that (our boss, our child, our neighbor, etc.) will never go along with that?" All of these create the same problems as *Why* questions, because they are about criticisms and defensive responses, not about asking true questions on how to *implement* the proposal.

▶ **Step 3: Respond with "Yes," "No," or "I'll think about it."**

Once you've heard a proposal and asked any questions you have about it, your next step is to simply respond with "Yes," "No," or "I'll think about it." You always have the right to say any one of these. Of course, each choice carries consequences, but you always have these three choices at least. Here are some examples of each:

Yes: "Yes, I agree. Let's do that." And then stop! No need to save face, evaluate the other person's proposal, or give the other person some negative feedback. Just let it go. After all, if you have been personally criticized or attacked, it's not about you. Personal attacks are not problem solving. They are about the person making the hostile attack. You are better off to ignore everything else. Of course, if your agreement on this issue will be recorded in writing, there may be more details to discuss—which may lead to more proposals.

No: "No, I don't want to change the pickup time. I'll try to make other arrangements to get there on time. Let's keep it as is." Just keep it simple. Avoid giving in to the urge to defend your decision or criticize the other person's idea. You said no, or used words to that effect, such as "That doesn't work for me." You're done. Let it go. Think about your next proposal.

I'll think about it: "I don't know about your proposal, but I'll think about it. I'll get back to you tomorrow about your idea. Right now I have to get back to work. Thanks for making a proposal." Once again, just stop the discussion there. Resist the temptation to discuss it at length or to question the validity of the other person's point of view. It is what it is.

When you say "I'll think about it," you are respecting the other person. It calms people to know you are taking them seriously enough to think about what they said. This doesn't mean you will agree. It just means you'll think about it. It helps to give a time when you will get back to the other person with your decision, such as "I'll get back to you tomorrow—or Friday by 5 p.m."

Make a New Proposal

If there isn't an agreement after using the three steps above, then the burden shifts to the respondent who said no. Now that person needs to make a new proposal. Perhaps the person will come up with a new approach that neither person thought of before. Encourage him or her to propose anything. (Remind them that there are consequences to each proposal.) And the other person involved can always respond with "Yes," "No," or "I'll think about it."

Bridge Proposals

If the individuals involved haven't made much progress after they have each made a proposal, then encourage them to really think about potential "bridge" proposals. As the name implies, these are proposals that will bridge, or connect, what each person has said is important in their proposals.

A Workplace Example

Most problems have many solutions that would work. For example, a workplace dispute arose between Jon and Jim over

Jon's loud phone calls in the cubicle next to Jim. Jim went to his manager to complain.

His manager was very busy and after a minute of hearing Jim's complaint, he asked Jim: "So, what's your proposal. How should we solve this problem?"

Jim said, "I don't know. Isn't that your job?"

His manager, trying not to get irritated, said, "Actually, you're the person closest to the situation, so I would be very interested in what solutions you might propose. I've also got a lot on my plate right now."

Jim thought a moment. "Well, I propose that you find a better cubicle for him, since he has so many phone calls that need to be made and I often hear them."

"That's one idea. Let me think about that. Actually, let's talk to Jon and see if he has any suggestions as well and then decide what to do," the manager replied. Together, they walked over to Jon's cubicle.

"I hear there's a problem with sound carrying over into Jim's cubicle. Do you have any suggestions for how it can be solved?" the manager asked Jon.

Jon glanced at Jim with an irritated look, but then sighed and said: "I guess I can try to make my phone calls when you're away from your cubicle. I know you're in and out. Are there any regular times that you're away each day?" His tone of voice was very reasonable.

Jim realized that he himself had sounded rather dramatic about the whole thing and that Jon was going to appear reasonable to their supervisor.

In as reasonable a voice as possible, Jim replied, "I suppose we could try that. But I really don't think you realize how distracting you can be."

"Okay," said their supervisor, looking at his watch. "So it's settled for now. Just try to do your best—both of you. Thanks for coming up with your own solution." And he walked off.

While it wasn't Jim's preferred solution, Jon did make an effort after their discussion to be quieter and to make most of his calls when Jim was away from his cubicle. Since the supervisor passed the burden of solving this problem back to Jim and Jon, Jim realized that he couldn't really complain any further about it for now.

Discussion of This Example

This example shows three key points: First, by asking Jim and then Jon for their proposals, the manager kept the responsibility for solving this problem closest to the people involved, who knew the most about it. Second, he did not have to take on solving this problem along with all his other responsibilities. Third, he calmed the conflict, because Jim—known for being dramatic and a complainer—now realized that he wasn't going to be able to complain any further about this issue, at least for a while.

If Jim is a high-conflict person, he may have tendencies to make other people responsible for solving his problems. When his manager took the approach of asking for his proposals, he kept the responsibility on Jim's shoulders for solving problems he was closest to. Of course, if Jim is a reasonable person and it was a case of bullying or harassment by Jon, the manager would have needed to get further involved in resolving the conflict. But this was a minor issue and dealing with it as he did kept is minor. Asking "So, what's your proposal?" can prevent many minor issues from growing into major ones.

Also, did you notice how quickly Jim shifted from challenging his manager to making a proposal after the manager said, "I would be very interested in what solutions you might propose." Jim went from saying, "Isn't that your job?" to proposing, "Well, I propose that you find a better cubicle for him." This entire shift likely happened in just 30 seconds.

Likewise, Jon quickly shifted his position when asked "Do you have any suggestions?" Although he glanced at Jim with an *irritated* look, he then *sighed and offered,* "I guess I can try to make my phone calls when you're away from your cubicle."

A Smoother Parenting Example

The following example shows the three proposal-making steps *after* both people have shifted to making proposals. They may or may not need a mediator once they have learned how to do this.

William and Natasha have a four-year-old daughter, Halle. They recently separated and have a hard time talking to each other, because they usually argue. However, they both love Halle and want the best for her; they have both been reading articles about how to create the best parenting plan. Now they need to decide how they will share parenting time with their daughter. They are going to meet with a family mediator to help them reach an agreement. Before the meeting, they are each to prepare a proposal.

Natasha has read that young children should have the stability of one primary parent, with the active involvement of the other parent. The article said this is especially true with children age three or older. William has read an article that recommended shared parenting—at least 35 percent for each parent and possibly a 50-50 schedule. The experts consulted for this article seemed to suggest that this arrangement works for children of any age.

They had heard that the best plan is always one that both parents can agree to. Also, the children should feel that their schedule is normal and routine, and that their parents aren't always stressed or fighting over the schedule. Neither William nor Natasha wants to keep fighting about this, but they both feel strongly about their different points of view.

Here are their initial proposals:

Natasha's first proposal: "*I read an article that says it's best for young children to have one primary household, but that the other parent is involved every week. So I propose that Halle live with me most of the time, but that she spends one day and overnight each* *week with you. In my proposal, you would also have half of the major holidays each year, and then we could alternate the following year."*

William's question: *"I have a question about your proposal. What day and overnight were you picturing that I would have each week?"*

Natasha: *"I was thinking you'd have Friday nights and all day Saturdays each week."*

William's response: *"Okay, I think I understand your proposal. I would say 'No' to that, as I read an article that says it's best for children to have approximately equal time with each parent."*

William's first proposal: *"I propose that Halle spend six days and nights with me in a two-week period, so you would have eight nights in the same period, as I recognize she's been with you more of the time up until now. After she's five, I'd like a 50-50 schedule, so this would be a transition."*

Natasha's question: *"Which nights were you thinking of having with her?"*

William: *"I'd like a weekday overnight every week—like Wednesdays—and I would alternate weekends, Friday at 5 p.m. through Monday morning back to daycare one weekend and Friday overnight the other weekend."*

Natasha's response: *"Well, my answer to that would be 'No.' I think she's way too young to be spending that much time away from me, as I've been her primary caregiver for all these years. And that just seems like too much back and forth for a girl that young. However, I might be willing to consider that she spend a little more time with you, especially as she gets older."*

William: *"But I want to be fully involved in her growing up— weekdays with her schoolwork as well as weekends. So here's another proposal . . ."*

Discussion of This Example

There are at least three possible proposals for William to make now. No one proposal is right for everyone's situation, and there is usually more than one workable solution to a problem. Here are a few options in this case:

Option 1: 3 nights/11 nights in two weeks
William's new proposal: *"I would agree to have three nights every two weeks. I would have Wednesdays overnight every week and Friday night and all day Saturday every other week."*

Option 2: 4 nights/10 nights in two weeks
William's new proposal: *"I would agree to have four nights every two weeks. I would have Wednesdays overnight every week and alternate weekends from Friday at 5 p.m. to Sunday at 5 p.m."*

Option 3: 5 nights/9 nights in two weeks
William's new proposal: *"I would agree to have five nights every two weeks. I would have Wednesdays overnight every week and alternate weekends from Friday at 5 p.m. to Monday back to daycare."*

Some parents would agree on option 1, some on option 2, and others on option 3. The reality is that there is not a huge difference between these options. William and Natasha could go back and forth asking questions of each other and making proposals until they reached an agreement—on their own or with the assistance of a mediator or other professional.

The idea is that the process of making proposals helps build an agreement that can work the best for the people involved. Be patient and creative, and you can probably arrive at a good solution.

Practice Exercise

I suggest using the above example as a practice exercise. You can do this with another person, or you can guide clients through this if you are a professional. Two people take the parts of William and Natasha and read it out loud, to get the flow or rhythm of making proposals, asking questions, and then responding. Then they can keep going after the script ends and try to reach an agreement with further proposals, questions, and responses.

Preparing Proposals

It's easy to make a proposal at any time. However, in some situations, it helps to prepare proposals in advance and possibly write them down. Consult with friends, family, and professionals to stay focused on problem solving, rather than blaming. Learn to ask questions. This is part of the Big Shift: Stay engaged in problem-solving activities so a possible HCP doesn't slip back into complaining and blaming.

Make a List

Another suggestion is to encourage the person or people involved to "make a list" of solutions for their situation. Making a list focuses people in their problem-solving brains, rather than their defensive brains because writing uses the right hand, which engages the left brain (left-handed people apparently engage both hemispheres while writing), as I said in the previous chapter.

What If Their Proposals Don't Go Anywhere?

Just asking "So, what's your proposal?" rarely solves the problem itself. However, it is a great starting point, because it shifts the person from blame to problem solving. Now, the issue is finding an agreeable proposal that they can both say "yes" to, like Emma and Jake finally did in the first chapter.

There are several possible approaches you can use when dealing with an individual in conflict with yourself, or when dealing with two or more people in conflict with each other. These will be demonstrated further in the examples in the following chapters.

1. "Deconstruct" their proposals. This involves asking questions about their proposals, including what it would look like. With this knowledge you can say, "It seems like what is most important to you is such and such. Is that correct?" Then you can explain what is most important to you. If you're facilitating a mediation, you can state what you hear is most important to each party and then ask, "Is that correct?" If it is not correct, you can ask what would be the more accurate description of their concerns.

2. Suggest at least three alternative approaches. Many people, especially high-conflict people, have little experience with a wide range of solutions to problems. They are used to fighting for only one solution without any flexibility—or they just give up. They make the conflict personal instead of looking for viable solutions. Here it often helps to suggest at least three solutions to similar problems that other people have used. For example, in a dispute over whether a business partner is hiding money, you could say:

A. "You could do more financial 'discovery' to see if there's any information that supports your side of the argument."

B. "You could bring more information to our next meeting and we can see if we are persuaded that the situation is as you say it is."

C. "We could proceed right now, with the information at hand."

3. Take a break for a week or two or three. It's common for stressful issues to lose their potency after people take a break. Indeed, a week or two—or three—often does wonders toward resolving a dispute. It gives people time to calm down, to research more options, and to ask more questions. Of course, some situations can't be put on hold for a week or more; in these cases, try taking a break for a day or as little 20 to 30 minutes.

4. Suggest that the people involved write down their outer limits ("bottom lines") for negotiating a settlement. Then they could give these to you confidentially, so the other person doesn't see what each other wrote. You can quickly scan these outer limits to determine whether or not it's likely that they will reach an agreement. Then say, "You should be able to reach an agreement from what I see—keep making proposals." Or, "It appears unlikely that you will reach an agreement. But I suggest you each make one last proposal just to see if there are any new ideas." I have had cases where the participants did make better final proposals than their notes indicated and eventually came to an agreement. This process also gets them out of defensive reacting and into logical problem solving.

5. *Recognize that it often takes HCPs two to three times longer than ordinary cases to reach an agreement.* It may seem hopeless to really help one or two of the parties reach an agreement. Yet they often are making small progress without realizing it. Because of the brain factors described in the previous chapter, they may have to process every conflict with defensive reacting first, then calm themselves down and use their logical problem solving second. This double process may be effective—it just takes longer.

6. *Tell them to think of two proposals for any unresolved problem.* By thinking of two proposals, it gets them off of fixed positions. HCPs especially have a tendency to lock into one position and then fight for it endlessly. Yet negotiators have known for decades that "positions" make it harder to negotiate, not easier. It's rare that one's initial position becomes the final agreement, so it's worthwhile to dream up more than one potential solution before you start making proposals. Expecting two proposals for each problem helps avoid fixed positions while not trying to persuade them to have insights about each other's interests, which often just frustrate them. They typically can't picture the other person having any valid interests.

7. *Help them discuss who is going to make the decision for them.* HCPs often threaten to quit negotiations and go to court instead. You can avoid "catching" their frustration and anger by leading a problem-solving discussion of what to do next. You can help them discuss several options, such as:

- Taking a break for a few weeks, and then meeting again
- Discussing what it would cost to go to court (HCPs usually have no idea)
- Hiring a private judge or expert to give an opinion; then they can negotiate based on that
- Bringing lawyers, accountants, friends, or others to another negotiation session
- Bringing written opinions from lawyers to the next negotiation session

By turning their impasse into just another problem-solving exercise, the people in conflict are more likely to come up with some other good ideas and possibly resolve their dispute during this discussion. I have seen it happen many times. It's as though the reasonableness and non-defensiveness of this discussion opens up clearer thinking—and more realistic thinking. Most people know that court can cost more and take longer than resolving a dispute out of court.

If it is not a court dispute, discussing alternatives can still help them focus logically. The key is that you, as a friend, manager, or mediator, can help them stay calm and focused on solutions by staying calm and focused on solutions yourself. You can avoid defensive reacting and joining in their frustration. By shifting them to logical problem solving, you can create a space in which they can make proposals rather than defending and attacking each other. And any obstacle they throw at you can be turned into just another problem to solve.

Summary

It isn't easy at first to stay calm and not feel responsible for someone else's upset, especially if the person is strongly blaming you. But it can be done by consciously reminding yourself of encouraging statements, such as the ones discussed above. It helps to remind yourself of such statements *before* you go into a potentially heated situation—it's like putting armor on before entering into battle.

Once you are calm yourself, you can ask the individual or people in conflict, "So, what's your proposal?" Then briefly explain how proposals are made. You can say:

There are just three simple steps for making proposals at any time: First, say Who would do What, When, and Where. Then, the other person can ask questions (being careful not to criticize the proposal or instantly respond), such as asking about how the first person's detailed picture of the proposal might be implemented if it was agreed upon. Lastly, the other person can say, "Yes," "No," or "I'll think about it." That's all—just a simple answer. There's no need to argue about a proposal. And if you say no to a proposal, then you get to make the next proposal. Any questions about that?

This explanation takes about 30 seconds. If you're someone in charge of a situation, such as a manager, a chairperson for a meeting, or a mediator, this explanation can quickly change the overall tone of a conflict or outbreak of anger or blaming. If it's just you and a complaining person, you can take more time to hear the person's upset feelings, but then still shift the focus to problem solving by coming up with proposals. You can encourage the person to ask you questions, to seek out others to ask for suggestions, or to make a list of problems and proposed solutions.

Lastly, by teaching how to make proposals in the heat of a conflict, you will help yourself stay calm and earn the respect of those around you.

CHAPTER FOUR

Dealing with Resistance

High-conflict people have a lot of resistance to logical problem solving. They start off in a defensive reaction and get stuck there:

"Why should I have to make a proposal? This is all your fault! You have to fix it!"

"Don't patronize me by telling me to make a proposal!"

"You know I can't solve this. You have to tell me what to do. I'll do whatever you say."

"You're not listening to me. You don't understand how horrible the situation really is."

"You're in charge! I have no idea how this can be solved. You have to get rid of people."

Avoiding Responsibility

High-conflict people tend to avoid responsibility and focus on blaming others. Did you notice that all of the strong statements above made the listener responsible while the speaker avoided responsibility? This seems to be because many HCPs have personality disorders or traits, and one characteristic of a personality disorder is that it makes the person constantly feel like a victim—helpless, vulnerable, and powerless. They truly do not see how they contribute to their own problems and you can't succeed at pointing this out to them, because they will become even more defensive with you and make it all your fault.

However, not all people with personality disorders or traits have a high-conflict personality. (See the diagram on page 50.) Only those who focus on blaming a specific person or group (their "targets of blame") seem to become HCPs. The rest of those with personality disorders just feel helpless and vulnerable without blaming anyone in particular. They rarely get involved in legal disputes or other prolonged conflicts. They often avoid conflict or avoid people—or both.

Overlap of HCPs & Personality Disorders

HCPs
• Preoccupied
with target(s)
of blame

Personality Disorders
• Interpersonal dysfunction
• Lack of self-awareness
• Rarely change behavior

Also, many HCPs don't have personality disorders, although they usually have some traits of these disorders. You will spot them by how frequently they deny all responsibility for their problems and claim helplessness. They don't see how they contribute to their own problems or their conflicts with others. This means they also don't feel responsible for solving conflicts.

Rather, they see conflict resolution as the job of other people—either the other parties to the conflict or the people in charge. They may become preoccupied with blaming people they are close to (such as boyfriends, girlfriends, husbands, wives, parents, children, close friends, or close co-workers) and those they see in positions of authority (such as supervisors, business owners, professionals, government officials, companies, or government agencies).

For these reasons, they have never developed conflict resolution skills for when they are upset. Interestingly, when they are not upset, they may be skilled at solving problems. Some HCPs are even doctors, lawyers, business owners, politicians, scientists, and others who must regularly deal with others' conflict. When they are focused on the task of their jobs, they can be brilliant (possible left-brain focus). It's only when they get into relationship conflicts or have to deal with a personal crisis that they become like three-year-olds and act in a very extreme manner (possible right-brain defensiveness).

Expect Resistance

With this in mind, their resistance to taking responsibility for problem solving—especially relationship problem solving—makes more sense. This resistance is part of their personalities; therefore, they don't recognize it and you shouldn't point it out to them. Just be aware that resistance can quickly surface when they are asked to take responsibility for solving problems, even with our simple question: "So, what's your proposal?"

While you may not be able to change the resistant part of their personalities, the way that you respond to it can make all the difference in the world. If you can remain calm and gently explain how simple it is to make proposals, you will usually meet some success.

I deal with this kind of resistance all the time in situations like the one sketched out in the first chapter. While Emma and Jake did not have high-conflict personalities, they did exhibit right-brain defensiveness. If someone gets regularly stuck in this defensiveness, then they may have high-conflict personalities and you should *expect* a lot of resistance from them. In these cases, just stay calm and repeatedly focus on how they can make proposals to resolve their own problems.

By showing that you will not take on responsibility for their problems or become defensive yourself, they will usually calm down—or leave you alone, out of frustration. Don't let their upset emotions make you in charge of their problems. Even if you're a family member or professional, you are not responsible for other people's problems—just for assisting them, at the most.

This means that you can take a supportive, educational role with upset people. You can tell them how they can ask questions, make lists, make proposals, and respond to proposals. You can assure them that they *can* do this. These are very simple tasks, and completing them often gives people a sense of pride.

Making Several Suggestions

One way to deal with resistance in others is to suggest several sample proposals they can make. A complaining person may truly have no idea how to solve a problem they are facing—or you are jointly facing. You can use your skill and knowledge to give them several options, especially if you have had prior experience in this area.

For example, a lawyer may be working with a client who is a partner in a small business that is closing. It was losing business and losing money, and the partners stopped getting along.

Client: "I think that we lost money because my partner was secretly taking money out of the business. He handled most of the financial record-keeping for the ten years of the business."

Lawyer: "Your business is in a market that's on the decline. Don't you think that it has something to do with that? And the accountant for the business says the books look clean. What makes you think that your partner was hiding money?"

Client: "I just thought we had more money in the bank than he says we do. He seems untrustworthy to me. It's just a feeling I have, but I wouldn't have that feeling if it wasn't true, don't you think? Can you demand to see all of our financial records and bring a legal action against him if you find something? You've got to do something!"

Lawyer: "Yes, I could do that. And I can understand your frustration that there doesn't seem to be a good explanation for why you are losing business and money. However, I still think it's possible that it's the economy rather than your business partner, since you didn't seem to have those concerns before the recent economic downturn. But this is up to you. I'll tell you some options that you have; then you can decide what you want to propose that we do. Here are three options:

1. I could subpoena all of the business bank account records.

2. Or, before that, you could bring in your accountant to sit down with you, me, your partner, and his lawyer, and explain the business finances to all of us.

3. Or, you could just accept that the business has less than you expected and assume that if your business partner really wanted to hide money, you probably will never find it.

So it's up to you. What do you propose?"

Client: "I don't know what to do. Why don't you decide? You're the lawyer."

Lawyer to himself: ("I'm not going to become responsible for his decision, because I know that he will blame me for it later. It's got to be his decision—his responsibility. There's no right answer here, except that it has to be his choice, not mine.")

Lawyer: "This is a decision that you're going to have to make. It's a very personal choice. I've had clients who wanted to go all the way with subpoenas and depositions and court hearings. Some have found money that was hidden, and in other cases we never found anything. Of course, this option costs the most, whether we find hidden money or not. Your relationship with your partner will also end in a fairly negative way if you go this route. He may be less flexible in how you divide up the known assets of the partnership.

"If you take the second approach, it might just help you understand more about how the business finances worked. Then, you can always decide if you want to proceed with subpoenas and depositions after that. Of course, it will cost you money and tension between you two if you proceed with questioning his financial management.

"If you take the third approach, you might be done pretty quickly and you can move on with your life. You won't have to spend much more on this, and you won't risk the cost of finding nothing. This could be the least expensive route."

Client: "I'm not sure what I should do. I just don't trust him. What would you advise?"

Lawyer to himself: ("Ordinarily, I would advise the second approach—the middle cost and risk. But I really hope that he chooses the third choice, so his case is over sooner. But I'm willing to work with him; this just has to be his decision because I think he's an HCP and I wouldn't be surprised if he blamed me—or sued me—for whichever approach I suggested we take. I have to keep the responsibility on his shoulders in this case.")

Lawyer: "As I said before, this is really a personal choice. I've given you some options and the costs and benefits of each. They all have pros and cons. Why don't you think about it and then call me and let me know what you propose. I'm willing to take any of these approaches, but you have to be the decision maker on this."

Client: "Actually, the more I think about it, the more I'm going to propose that we do the second choice—have the accountant come in and explain it to all of us. I would just be too upset with myself if I didn't at least look into my suspicions more deeply."

Lawyer: "I respect your decision and your thoughtfulness in making it. I'll get in touch with the other side and we can set up such a meeting. I'll also be sending you a letter confirming your decision today and the options that we weighed. Let's see what we find out!"

Discussion of This Example

We don't know whether the client is an HCP or not. But the lawyer seemed to have enough experience with him to be concerned. One general type of HCP is very suspicious of those close to them. The lawyer knew that if the client was suspicious of his business partner for ten years that sooner or later he might become suspicious of his lawyer. This is because HCPs tend to repeat their narrow patterns of relationship behavior with each new relationship.

Yet, by keeping the decision making on the client's shoulders, the lawyer can proceed with the *client's decision,* especially because he is going to put it in writing as the client's decision. Even if the client becomes angry later on about something, the lawyer has legally protected himself. And he is actually helping this client. Caution doesn't have to mean avoiding HCPs altogether. Plus, there's too many in the world to successfully avoid them all. But avoiding responsibility for their decisions is one part of managing a good relationship with an HCP.

Why didn't the lawyer just make one recommendation and leave it at that? The lawyer could have done that and would have been within his rights as a lawyer to give advice. As you could see by the lawyer's comments to himself, he thought the second option was the best choice, but he didn't want it to come from him or it would have reinforced the idea that it was his decision rather than his client's. This would have opened himself up to being blamed by the HCP if anything (even very minor) went wrong.

When you make just one recommendation and something— anything—goes wrong, an HCP will say that it was your decision and that you forced it on him or her. And things often go wrong in the minds of HCPs, because they constantly feel like victims— helplessness, vulnerable, and powerless—regardless of what is really happening. This, too, is just part of their personality. The lawyer in this example simply took the cautious approach. From his experience, this was an important part of working with such clients.

Why didn't the lawyer just fire the client and get out of the case, since he already thought that his client was an HCP? There are several factors for lawyers to consider in such a situation. If there was a court hearing or other legal action already scheduled, lawyers have an ethical responsibility not to "abandon" their clients. But whether or not any paperwork had been filed with the court to dissolve the client's business partnership, the lawyer may have been familiar with handling cases with HCPs and knew how to make it work. There are many legal cases involving HCPs, and many lawyers who have learned to handle these clients well. That is how this case was described.

This wasn't really about making a proposal, was it? The client was actually making the decision. Yes, but the lawyer took the approach of calling the decision a proposal. That left him a little wiggle room if he chose not to do what the client proposed. He simply agreed with the *client's proposal* of using the second option and then treated it as the *client's decision.*

In general, if someone who's upset can't think of a proposal, offer more than one option for them to consider. That way they can't say it was your decision and blame you for it later. And if it's a potentially legal situation, provide a written summary of how the decision was made—such as in a follow-up letter—which shows that you offered several options and the person made the final decision.

It's Up to You

Did you notice how the lawyer in the above example emphasized that the proposal/decision was up to the client? "But this is up to you." "So it's up to you. What do you propose?" "I'll tell you some options that you have; then you can decide." "You have to be the decision maker on this." While this may seem redundant, it is necessary with HCPs, as they often don't remember what you said the first few times.

Since this message is particularly important, it needs repeating. This is also why putting the decision and the process in writing can be a good idea. When people are under stress (anyone, not just HCPs), they don't remember very well. In difficult situations, people are mostly in their right-brain defensiveness and their left-brain problem-solving memories may not be connected.

Dancing with the Resistance

Did you notice that the lawyer showed some empathy for the client's concerns, even though he was doubtful about them?

"Yes, I could do that. And I can understand your frustration that there doesn't seem to be a good explanation for why you are losing business and money." Then, he went on to educate the client about his options. This is the two-step approach I call "Dancing with the Resistance." It involves stepping toward and leading a person, as in a dance:

1. You step toward the person with a statement, showing empathy or respect for their concerns.

2. Then, you try to lead the person toward you by educating them on the issue.

They are much more likely to hear what you have to say if you show interest in their viewpoint. Remember, if you are aggressive or discounting of their concerns, they are likely to slip into their right-brain defensiveness and get stuck there. On the other hand, when you can acknowledge and show empathy for their concerns ("I can understand your frustration"), you help them stay calm.

Of course, you have to train yourself to do this—it's not natural. You are more likely to feel like criticizing them or getting angry yourself. "How could you say such a thing?" "Do you know how stupid that sounds?" Instead, stay calm and try to connect with their confusion and frustration. They didn't ask to have the problems they have, and they don't see how they contribute to them. None of this is obvious. So try to help them rather than judge them.

What about Identifying Interests?

The above example shows someone resisting the idea of making a proposal and having no idea what their proposal might be. But you might also encounter HCPs who have very strong ideas about what they want and have taken adamant positions on an issue. Indeed, this is very common with HCPs, who don't typically seek advice from others but instead tell others what to do. They do this a lot with lawyers, counselors, mediators, supervisors, customer service representatives, and others.

Many dispute resolvers have been trained to do "interest-based" negotiations, rather than bargaining from "positions." For thirty years, negotiation experts have emphasized that "interest-based" negotiating is much more satisfying and effective than "position-based" bargaining. The classic book on this subject is *Getting to Yes: Negotiating Agreement without Giving In*, by Fisher and Ury, which came out over thirty years ago.

Yet, identifying each other's interests at the beginning of negotiations is usually too hard for people with high-conflict personalities. They have difficulty recognizing that the other person could possibly have any legitimate interests, and they lack the insight into themselves to identify their own interests. Instead, they usually come into a situation ready to demand or argue for one solution, which they might actually call their "position." Rather than arguing with them about not having positions, it's much easier to simply say, "That's a proposal. We're going to get to proposals very soon. Proposals are what eventually lead to agreements."

If they argue that their solution has to be accepted and that it's not "just a proposal," you can say, "That's fine. You might be right. It might become your final agreement. But it really helps to have a full discussion of several proposals before reaching a final agreement, if you want it to last." Usually, people accept that—because you haven't rejected their "proposal" and you've cast it in a good light.

Remember in chapter 3, I suggested that you "deconstruct" their proposals to find their interests and then tell them what you see "is important to both of you in your proposal(s)." This is a way for you to identify their interests without trying to get them to recognize each other's interests, since HCPs have a very hard time with that.

Often, however, you don't need to do this because their proposals lead to discussions on the details of what can be done in the future, rather than needing to discuss their past concerns and preferences (interests). I have been involved in numerous cases where interests were not discussed, yet agreements were made that satisfied both parties.

It's not that interests are unimportant; it's that HCPs have so much resistance to the idea of interests and analyzing them. They don't think that they have interests—they just think that they're right. And they can't accept that the other person could have valid interests, so focusing on interests just starts an unnecessary fight.

Summary

High-conflict people tend to avoid responsibility for problem solving when there is a conflict with someone else. On one hand, they resist even making proposals, claiming that this is the responsibility of others or they just don't know how to do this. On the other hand, they may approach a problem with one all-or-nothing solution and fight hard for it. In both approaches, they resist participating in the process of solving problems.

Yet you can assist them in finding realistic solutions by teaching them the process of making proposals—and by working *with* their resistance rather than *against* it. You can take a two-step "dance with the resistance" by (1) acknowledging their concerns and showing empathy or respect for them, and (2) educating them about alternative ways of solving the problem.

If you can ride out the storm of resistance to making proposals, you can actually help people—even high-conflict people—solve their problems and feel good about it. Besides, it's *their* decision and solution, not someone else's. If decisions come partially from their own proposals, they tend to stick with them and even fight for them—rather than resist them, which is so common with HCPs.

The Following Chapters

In order to help you lessen resistance, the following chapters show you how to be flexible in the way you approach the other person or people, including the terms you use and the way you make proposals yourself. Again, the goal is to shift upset, potentially HCPs into *flexible thinking* and away from their defensive *all-or-nothing thinking*. To see how all the following chapters help with this overall concept, here is a chart of how these approaches influence people and problem solving. The remaining chapters demonstrate these principles in many different settings.

Relationship Negotiation Styles

FLEXIBLE THINKING	ALL-OR-NOTHING THINKING
Making proposals: "Here's my proposal." Asking for proposals: "So, what's your proposal?"	Making demands: "It's my way or the highway!" Shutting out all other opinions and options.
Accepting a flexible response to a proposal: "Yes," "No," or "I'll think about it."	Accepting only total agreement with a demand.
When first proposals are not accepted, getting active in seeking more information and ideas.	When first proposals are not accepted, getting angry and rigidly repeating original demand.
Other words: Options, alternatives, lists, preferences, choices, requests.	Other words: "You *have to* do it this way." "You have *no choice*." "You've *trapped* me; *I* have no choice."
Educating about consequences.	Ignoring the consequences.
Careful to evoke a positive response in the other person. Realizes power to influence other person.	Careless about evoking a negative response in the other person. Unaware of influence on the other.

CHAPTER FIVE

Brainstorming at Work

Throughout much of history, jobs have been structured in a primarily hierarchical, top-down way. Roles and rules were clear-cut and, as workers, we only had to follow them—to "do our job." In recent years, however, with the success of technology and education, society is rapidly changing and many relationships are becoming much more equal and collaborative.

Nowhere is this more evident than in the workplace and the business world. The rules are in flux and the roles are very fuzzy. There is constant need for—and opportunity for—negotiating successful relationships with many people: customers, co-workers, supervisors, partners, owners, and others. However, this means that everyone needs to learn and practice good negotiation skills on a daily basis. This is both a frightening and an exciting time of possibility for those with the ability to learn. An essential part of this process is learning how to make and respond to proposals.

Jessica's Challenge

For managers, this evolving strategy means bringing out the best ideas and efforts of team members while still leading the team in meeting its goals. Finding the right balance of what's negotiable and what's not is very important—especially with today's employees who want respect, flexibility, and opportunities to share their ideas.

Jessica is in her thirties and just became one of the youngest department heads in her company. One of her older employees, Sam, had also applied for her job. She was concerned about how to establish herself and her role as department head—and how to deal with this employee who was already expressing doubt in her competence to other employees.

To begin building strong relationships with her employees and because they often worked off-site, she decided to meet with each of them individually This would also help her manage any possible HCPs, as she knew it would be important to "connect" with HCPs as well as lay the groundwork for setting limits and getting the most out of them by welcoming their proposals.

Following is a discussion she had during one of her first relationship-building meetings with Sam:

Jessica: "Sam, you're one of the first team members I wanted to meet with, since you have the most experience in this department. I'm very interested in your perspective, and I want you to know that I welcome everyone's proposals for how to deal with any problems that arise. Actually, I am asking everyone to tell me one or two proposals—or "options"—for solving any problem that they bring to my attention.

"Now, tell me how you came to work here and what you think will be some of our biggest challenges this next quarter."

Sam: "Well, getting product A out on the market is going to be a huge problem. We've been working on it for three years. I've been personally working on it from Day One. I'm the only one still here who has this much experience on it."

Jessica: "That's great! You'll be a major team resource. But before we talk about product A, I'd really like to hear what attracted you to this company. Was it product A? Or what came before that? I'd really like to know more about the company's history and culture."

By deciding what topic they're going to discuss and when, Jessica is teaching Sam that she is in charge of the conversation. But she is also demonstrating her interest in having a strong working relationship with him and that she values his perspective on the company and on product A. This is part of her "two-step" dance with him: (1) connecting with his point of view and concerns, and then (2) leading him in the direction she wants: getting the best proposals that he can give her, even if he's difficult. This will help her manage him and benefit from his experience.

Sam explains what attracted him to the company. From this discussion, Jessica learns that he really likes detail work and that he really wants to be respected. In general, Sam doesn't feel that the company has given him enough recognition for his contributions. Jessica sees that respect is a very important issue for him. Therefore, she realizes that she will need to regularly acknowledge his contributions, while discouraging any tendencies he may have to feel superior to the other employees or entitled to special treatment.

Jessica: "That's really interesting. You're quite a resource. Now, let's talk about product A. I hear there are some problems with it that may hold us back from our planned release date in three months."

Sam, now irritated: "Who said that? There's no problem. It's going to be a great product, if you'll just get it out there. The public is going to love this new device. But our competitors are also working hard on a similar product, so we have to get ours out first! You have to make it happen!" He was becoming demanding in a surprising way that Jessica found intimidating. She couldn't let this happen. More two-step.

Jessica: "Yes, I agree with you that we want to get it out as soon as possible. However, I also know that it can backfire if we launch before the product is truly ready. Remember how Obama's health care website launch created more problems than it solved, because it wasn't ready and he was quite embarrassed by it."

Sam: "Yes, but remember Steve Jobs of Apple. He also rushed out products and grabbed the market before anyone even knew there even was a market—for iPods, iPhones, and iPads. I've worked with people from Apple and I know how they work. You have to be fast—very fast—and not afraid. You're not afraid of failure, are you?" Sam asked, narrowing his eyes. Jessica could tell that he wanted to see if he could push her around.

Jessica: "Well, I appreciate your knowledge and drive. We're going to have a meeting the day after tomorrow, and I want you to bring your best proposals for what we should do. I'm going to hear from everyone, then decide how we should move forward. I'm encouraging everyone to do their own brainstorming alone first; then we'll share ideas and see where it takes us."

Sam: "That's ridiculous! Everyone knows that you do brainstorming together, not alone."

Jessica: "Actually, you may not be aware of it, but the research coming out now indicates that brainstorming *alone first* is more effective than brainstorming together from the start. When groups brainstorm from the start, a few people tend to dominate the group's thinking and it discourages others from being as creative—they are too heavily influenced by the few and it narrows the group's thinking prematurely. I want the widest range of ideas before I decide which way we're going to go. So see what proposals you can come up with. Several proposals, without judging them yet, would be great."

Sam: "If you insist," he grumbled.

Brainstorming Alone versus in Groups

As Jessica said, there is research now (and has been for years, actually) that shows brainstorming alone is freer and more creative than group brainstorming. It avoids the issues of peer pressure and fear of criticism for "bad" ideas. In her book *Quiet: The Power of Introverts in a World That Can't Stop Talking,* author Susan Cain explains that forty years of research has shown that brainstorming when alone generates more and better ideas than group brainstorming sessions. In fact, the larger the group, the less creative the results.

Yet companies keep brainstorming in groups. Why? Because it makes people feel good and more "attached" as a group. The downside? They believe they are more creative than they really are.

However, Cain did note that recent research shows *online brainstorming* in groups is better than individual brainstorming. Here the larger the group, the better they are at it. She mentions Linux and Wikipedia as examples of online large group brainstorming that have been generally successful.

Cain gives three reasons for the limited success of in-person group brainstorming, but I believe a fourth category needs to be added involving high-conflict people. Here are her three reasons:

- "Social loafing"—groups provide cover for loafers while others do the work.

- "Production blocking"—only one can speak at a time, so others have to wait.

- "Evaluation apprehension"—some would-be contributors fear public criticism (even though the standard rules for brainstorming say that all ideas are fair game, even silly ones).

To these, I would add the following when high-conflict people are involved:

- HCPs drive to dominate the group—HCPs can be very aggressive, so they try to take over the groups they are in. Many consider brainstorming a competitive sport.

- Others give up—those who work with an HCP often save their energy for other matters, rather than competing to be heard when the HCP wants all the attention.

- HCPs often seek revenge or vindication—co-workers quickly learn that HCPs who take something the wrong way can make their lives miserable with blaming or secret sabotage, and brainstorming is so unstructured that HCPs can easily be offended if their ideas are revised or replaced by someone else's ideas.

- Managers often focus too much on HCPs—in an effort to effectively manage HCPs, many managers give them extra attention: either trying to explain things patiently to them or engaging in power struggles with them so they can allow others to participate.

Managing HCPs with Proposals

While individual brainstorming first is one way to neutralize these problems, another is to emphasize that they are proposals, not decisions. A manager can guide a discussion away from a dominating HCP by saying, "I need more proposals before we go further with that idea." Or, if an HCP is getting defensive about someone else's brainstorming idea: "It's just a proposal, so there's no need to respond to it. Just give me another proposed idea."

The mistake that many managers and co-workers make with HCPs is engaging them in a logical argument in an effort to convince them to think or act differently. This just doesn't work with HCPs who lack the self-awareness to reflect on their own behavior. Efforts to persuade them to reject their past behavior only increase their defensiveness and counterattacks. Save your energy and focus on the future—by asking for proposals.

Don't give the HCP extra airtime. Just say you need to hear proposals from others. It's not a rejection of their ideas, because it's just a proposal. Proposals are neither good nor bad when made; they're just building blocks that may or may not get used in constructing the final plan. They all contribute to the pile from which we will build solutions.

Sam's Proposals

Jessica announced that the meeting about product A would be a conference call, because two key team members were going to be out of town. To reduce any negative effects of group brainstorming, she decided to conduct the meeting over the phone rather than through a video conference. If people couldn't see each other, perhaps no one person could dominate or intimidate the group. There were five key team members involved. Here's how the conference call played out:

Jessica: "Product A is behind schedule and we have a planned release date in three months. I'd like to get your best ideas and proposals for what we should do. Who wants to go first with their suggestions?"

Sam: "We should put it out, regardless of how perfect is it. It's a decent product and we can improve it after it's out. Time is of the essence, because of our competitors."

Tony: "It's not even decent yet. We will embarrass ourselves if we get it out prematurely. We still have miles to go on making it do everything we promised. Sure, it's functional right now, but it's not up to our usual standards. Releasing it like this could hurt our credibility."

Sam: "How can you say it's not even decent yet? I've been working on this for three years and it's sure as hell satisfactory!"

Jessica: "I prefer we not debate any specific proposals or exact words at this point. Let's just keep coming up with proposals for what to do. What do you think, Carly?"

Carly: "I think we should delay the release date until it's fully functioning. Although we could squeak by right now, I wouldn't be proud of it. In today's tech world, people lose interest fast. They could say, 'Guess that didn't meet expectations. Who's making a better one?'"

Sam: "That's absurd. You all know that no one else is anywhere near producing a product like product A. It's unique and special. We should get it out as planned, and then improve it. Plus, there's a lot we can do in three months if everyone knows we have a deadline to keep. If we extend the deadline, people—our people—will get lazy."

Jessica: "Is that your proposal, Sam? That we rush ahead during the next three months and release it in whatever shape it's in?"

Sam: "Actually, I have another proposal. I did a little research on how Steve Jobs released his biggest products. I propose that we announce it in three months with a big publicity event, then put it on the market three to six months later. Jobs announced his products this way to get a jump on the publicity and to get the market hungry to see it. He did that with the iPhone—he announced it in January 2007 and didn't put it on the market until June. He announced the iPad in January 2010 and it went on sale in April—after a hubbub of criticism, because no one really knew what to expect. An iPad was a foreign concept back then. But he demonstrated each of these products on the day he announced them, so he could show off their best qualities, without mentioning the capacities that weren't finished yet. Since no one had it in their own hands, they couldn't know that it wasn't really functional yet, and they didn't have time to try to imitate it. But they really wanted to see it."

Jessica: "That's a great proposal, Sam. Something to really think about. Anyone else? Fred?"

Fred: "I like it. I like Sam's proposal. I think it's the compromise that might actually work: Announce it in three months, by which time we should know the date it will be ready to go on the market. Show what a model does, then tell everyone when it will go on sale. We'll just act like everything's normal—and we'll generate a lot of excitement. I think we can get a model ready to demonstrate most of what it can do within the next three months. We'll put everything into the model now, then into production as soon after that as possible. It really is coming along."

Jessica: "This idea does sound appealing. Let's think about it for a couple days before making a final decision. Please send me any further thoughts you have about this, so we can make the best decision. But I'm excited! Great proposal, Sam. I'm glad you looked for more than one proposal for today. And everyone else too! Thanks for your good thinking."

Discussion of This Example

Jessica got what she wanted: good ideas from Sam, without letting him railroad the group or get stuck in one proposal. She made sure to praise the behavior she wanted—that he made more than one proposal and that he actually came up with one of the best ideas. Even though Sam was an HCP in her mind, he had skills and knowledge that she needed. Rather than criticizing his rigidity and past actions, which would have just increased his defensiveness and made him much harder to manage, Jessica was learning to manage his behavior by focusing him on making proposals about the future and respecting him when he did.

Passive-Aggressive Behavior

One of the concerns that often comes up when dealing with high-conflict people is that of passive-aggressive behavior. It is very common with HCPs. For example, what if Sam didn't think of a proposal before the team meeting and refused to contribute a proposal. He might say: "Oh, I didn't have time," when in fact you suspect that he just didn't want to do what he was told. Perhaps this would be his passive-aggressive way of resisting Jessica's leadership, without admitting it.

In general, passive-aggressive behavior is really aggressive behavior that is denied. In such a case, being really clear about when and where certain tasks are to be done often helps. That way, you can simply say: "I guess you missed the deadline, so let's discuss what your choices now." That way, a whole work group is not stymied by an HCP and can move forward. Giving passive-aggressive behavior a lot of attention tends to increase it.

It's better to focus on what to do now, rather than arguing about what he should have done. There are choices and there are consequences. Just implement them and move on, without rewarding the misbehavior with extra attention or showing that you are visibly frustrated. That can be secretly (or openly) satisfying to an HCP.

The Best Surgeon

"Audrey!" shouted Dr. Acer at the entrance to the nursing supervisor's office. "You have to do something about your nurses. They're incompetent!"

"Dr. Acer," replied Audrey Standish, the nursing supervisor, "come in. Come in. Tell me what's happening."

"Your nurses aren't doing what I've told them to do in the surgical unit! I've told them over and over again."

"Here, have a seat. Let me get out a notepad. What do you want the nurses to know?"

"When I'm doing surgery on a patient, they are not to stand on my side of the patient. That's my side and it needs to be wide. And they need to stop asking questions when I ask them to get something. Just get it—no questions asked. Some of these idiots don't seem to know the simplest thing about where the pads, the wipes, the different instruments are. They don't even understand what they're called! You've got to do something!"

"Wow! Sounds like you're really stressed out. Here, use my notepad. Why don't you make a list of what you want them to do. The nurses tell me they'll do whatever you want. But they do say that they don't always know what you want—that they think you might not have said what you want when you think you have—because you're so focused on the surgery, of course. So make a list of what you want."

Dr. Acer started angrily writing his complaints on the notepad. As he was writing, he became less and less angry.

"You know, I've just thought of some really good ideas here. I don't think that I've written them down anywhere before. This is helpful. So you say that the nurses will do what I want?"

"Yes, as long as you tell them what that is. They really want to make your job easier, and many of them have lots of surgical nursing experience. If they could have a list of reminders they could see before they entered the surgical unit, that would really make things easier for them and for you. I know the hospital really values your work here, and we want to do everything we can to help. I know you've handled some incredible surgeries lately. I even saw one in the news."

"Yes, it's nice to get the recognition after all these years. But I don't want your nurses to sabotage me and get in the way. They have to be able to move fast sometimes. You know, it's a matter of life and death—the kind of work that I do."

"Yes, of course! I have another idea that might help. You've found it helpful to write this list here. I could also put a suggestion box somewhere near the O.R. and you could feel free to drop suggestions into it at any time. The nurses are really willing to do almost anything in order to help you focus on your work and stay calm."

"Yeah, that's a good idea. Listen, I've got to go now. Make sure your nurses see my instructions."

"Sure thing. Take care," Audrey said.

Discussion of This Example

Dr. Acer was angry. Audrey Standish knew that this doctor was likely a high-conflict person. He saw himself as superior to everyone else, even the other surgeons. Yet it's true that he brought in several million dollars a year in surgeries for the hospital and was respected in his profession. The nursing supervisor knew that the hospital wanted Dr. Acer to be happy.

On the other hand, Audrey knew that several nurses refused to work with Dr. Acer because he was so difficult and easily angered. Was he truly an HCP?

He was easily angered (unmanaged emotions) about things the other surgeons discussed calmly.

He had all-or-nothing thinking—the nurses were "incompetent" in his eyes, despite all of their training and experience.

He had extreme behavior—pushing them away from "his side" of the patient on the operating table, when where they stood did not affect his actual surgery.

He often blamed others, especially the nurses who worked the closest to him.

He exhibits the four basic characteristics of high-conflict people. But remember, it's not a diagnosis. Since Audrey suspected he was an HCP, she was wise to take the approach she did.

The nurses didn't disagree that he was a skilled surgeon, but he treated them so badly that they couldn't stand it. Dr. Acer had no clue how they felt about him. He was more focused on his successes and his own perceived stresses.

When Audrey focused him on writing a list that she had started based on his complaints, he shifted gears within a matter of seconds. He calmed himself by writing the list—and came up with some helpful suggestions! This is an example of how you can influence another person to act calmly by asking them to write a list or make a proposal. Even though the doctor was visibly upset, making a list proved to be a calming exercise for him.

Of course, this problem never would have been resolved if Audrey had gotten angry back at him in defense of her nurses. She helped them more by working with the doctor. She believed it would be better to calm him down, to help him make a list, and then to take stronger action if necessary. But the Big Shift seemed to work, and now they have new ideas for how to handle problems in the future, such as the suggestion box. She asked him to make proposals (the list) and she also offered her own proposal (the suggestion box). This story demonstrates how quickly people can calm down when focusing on proposals, even in the fast-paced setting of a hospital surgery department. What's more, Audrey was able to get Dr. Acer to write his list and agree to her proposal of a suggestion box all while maintaining a very casual and informal demeanor.

Making Your Own Proposal

In this case, Audrey was in the role of a colleague, rather than an employee of Dr. Acer, but her role in the organization was certainly below his. When you are an employee, you are in a harder position to say, "So, what's your proposal?" to a supervisor. Sometimes you can do that, depending on your relationship. But if your supervisor is an HCP, it may be misinterpreted as sounding disrespectful no matter what tactic you try. So you may be better off making your own proposal—and then asking for permission to do it, such as "Is that okay with you?" That saves your supervisor from having to think too much, while still feeling in charge. And you can't really be accused of insubordination. You were just making a proposal. Also, asking for permission in making a proposal to an HCP allows the HCP to feel respected, if not in control.

This also shifts the conversation from attacking you to problem solving. When you make a proposal, your supervisor may move into his or her problem-solving brain, rather than defensive-reacting brain—because you are not reinforcing defensiveness with your behavior. If you were to get defensive back, it would reinforce the existing tone of the conversation and probably keep your supervisor in a defensive mode. Better to focus on problem solving—even if you have to be the one making the proposal.

Summary

Whether you are a manager, a colleague, or an employee, proposals can get you through the day with anyone you deal with—HCP or not. They can help you avoid arguing or giving in when you are dealing with an upset customer, obnoxious co-worker, bullying supervisor, or challenging business partner.

If you're a manager, asking your team to suggest proposals will make your job easier and less stressful. Too many new managers take on too many of their employees' complaints and problems. Give these back to them as dilemmas to solve, based on their frontline experience and knowledge—and proposals.

If you're an employee, do as much brainstorming on your own as you can, and suggest that your co-workers do the same. Coming in to work with more than one proposal will help you avoid feeling overwhelmed if your first proposal is rejected in a group brainstorming session—especially in the rude manner many HCPs use. And if your HCP is your boss, do the brainstorming for your boss but let him or her still feel in charge.

An added benefit of asking for and making proposals at work is that you may earn the respect of those around you. Rather than getting defensive (as so many people do these days), you can stay calm and friendly as you simply ask, "So, what's your proposal?" or "Here's a proposal—is that okay with you?" Your sense of confidence in the face of conflict can be very impressive.

The more people who use this approach at work, the less defensive environment our workplaces will be for all of us.

CHAPTER SIX

Choices in Education

Proposals imply choices. Choices imply respect. And one of the biggest things students of all ages want is respect. When you offer the other person your proposals, it means that you realize you are giving him or her a choice. And when you ask, "So, what's your proposal?" you are making the other person aware that you know *you* have a choice—that you won't be pushed around.

This chapter will address how making proposals and asking for proposals can help students in different age groups, as well as their parents, teachers, and administrators.

Coping with Pressures and HCPs

The anxiety level of today's children is higher than that of children in psychiatric treatment in the 1950s. By the 1990s the average college student was more anxious than 71 percent of the college students in the 1970s, according to Jean M. Twenge and W. Keith Campbell, the authors of *The Narcissism Epidemic: Living in the Age of Entitlement*. These comparisons were made *before* the attacks of 9/11. Many indicators suggest that students are even more stressed today.

While much of this is beyond any one person's control, there are many predictable areas of pressure and conflict in education today where we do have the potential to gain control in dealing with others—including skills that can be taught for managing situations with high-conflict people at school. And since HCPs are increasing at a younger and younger age, today's children need skills in dealing with pressures *and* HCPs that their parents may not have needed in the past:

- Elementary school children have more bullies to deal with.
- Middle school and high school students have cyberbullies, exposure to Internet pornography, and abuse of their own photos and misdeeds in the form of "sexting."
- College students have less certain career choices, lower earning potential than their parents, and a higher percentage of HCPs in their dating pool.
- Graduate students have higher debts, more competition for jobs, and more potential HCPs in positions of power over their futures.

That's just the stress on students. Then there's the stress on parents, who are competing with the Internet and role models of bad behavior, while also dealing with divorce, mental health problems in their children (perhaps 25 percent of today's teenagers), job changes or losses, increased costs for higher education (if that is even an option), and being blamed by society for everything that's wrong with kids today.

Then, there are the teachers, who have to deal with an increasing number of HCP students who challenge them in class, break the rules, bully other students, and don't listen to their instructions. They also may get less support from some parents these days, who are uninvolved or overinvolved in their children's education. Yet, everyone's expectations are higher today for individual teachers to "perform" and prove that their students are learning.

Then there are more HCP parents to deal with, who may undermine the teacher's discipline and study requirements, or blame the teacher for everything that's "wrong" with their child. And, of course, today's teachers have to deal with parents who are going through high-conflict separations or divorces, including fighting over the child at school or trying to eliminate the other parent's contact with the school.

And let's not forget about the administrators—from elementary school principals to university presidents—who must satisfy the high expectations of a wide range of stakeholders. They are a particular magnet for HCPs, because HCPs tend to attack those in positions of authority, and administrators appear to have the most authority in school settings.

How can making proposals and asking for proposals help with all of these problems? We'll look at some examples in different age groups.

The "Bully"

Some elementary school students already demonstrate signs of having high-conflict personalities—they break the rules, assault or intimidate other students, and talk back to teachers and staff. But, of course, that's also what children do as they grow up and learn the limits of their aggressive social behavior. So calling a child a "bully" may be just as inappropriate as calling one an HCP. In fact, many children exhibit the behavior of both bullies and victims, so it can be hard to tell who "bullied" whom. In general, we don't think of people as having a personality disorder until they're adults, as most children show signs of extreme behavior—emotions and thinking—on their way to becoming balanced, responsible adults.

Bullying is defined as a pattern of aggressive behavior (not just one incident) intended to intimidate a person with lesser power or status. Overall, bullying behavior needs to be restrained and changed, especially while children are young. It can be hard on other students to see this behavior, because they are still learning the rules and boundaries, and they often mimic high-conflict behavior when there aren't sufficient restraints present. They also need to learn how to defend themselves against such behavior and how to be good citizens.

Let's consider an example here. Suppose that Annie is being hassled by Tony in her third-grade class. No one else is around.

Tony tells Annie, "You're just stupid. No one likes you. Give me your snack!"

Annie feels helpless and gives Tony her snack. She hates herself for doing that, but she was afraid of him. A lot of children who get bullied are afraid to "confront the bully," and this makes them feel worse about themselves. They don't feel strong enough for a confrontation, so if their parents tell them to fight back, they feel trapped: It's too scary to challenge the bully and it's overwhelming to challenge their parents. Bullies see this self-doubt and often increase their bullying, because they believe they have a willing victim.

But another approach is to teach children that they have choices—and so does the bully. They can tell themselves that it is the bully—not themselves—who is choosing to act badly and that they have the right to *choose* how to respond. If it doesn't feel safe to fight back or say something challenging, they can choose to tell themselves, "He's acting badly, not me. I don't have to agree with him. I have choices. I can think that he's an idiot even if I don't say it out loud."

Now, suppose Annie gets some practice at home making proposals and responding to proposals. Her parents allow her to say "No" or "I'll think about it" from time to time. In dealing with intimidating behavior, her parents have taught her that she has choices. Sometimes, to protect herself, Annie may just do what the bully says. Other times, she may say something and challenge the bully. She is not required to speak up and confront the bully, but she can always tell herself she has choices and that the bully is not respecting her choices.

Feeling that you have choices can increase your confidence. It's *your choice* to confront the bully—or not. You haven't given any power to the bully over you. Another choice is to resist the bully without directly confronting him. Let's look at how this could work for Annie:

Tony says, "You're just stupid. No one likes you. Give me your snack!"

Annie thinks to herself, *I've got choices. I can choose to say, "No. Leave me alone."* So that's what she says.

But suppose Tony now says, "How dare you say no to me!" Then he takes a swing to punch her in the nose.

Annie backs away a little, but firmly says what her parents have told her: "If you hit me, you'll be in big trouble!" Tony says, "What? You're really stupid." And, with that, he walks away. He doesn't punch her in the nose. He doesn't know what to think of what Annie just said, but she didn't act intimidated. It was her sense of confidence that she had choices—and he had choices—that made him leave her alone.

Of course, she should also be taught to run away and get help if she felt in serious danger. Or to say nothing and protect her face. These are all choices that only she can make in the moment. But if Annie is trained in making these choices, it can help her feel better about herself and not get stuck believing there's something wrong with her, a message that bullies often try to convey. It's her choice and her parents taught her they would respect whichever choice she made when dealing with a bully.

The Angry Parent

One day an angry mother confronted Ms. Garcia about her fifth-grade son's poor grades on his first report card. Ms. Garcia felt like telling the mother, "If you would make sure that he gets his homework done, he might get better grades." After all, Ms. Garcia had suggested that all the parents help their children remember to do their homework, and she sent home instructions with the students once a week. This mother was one of the most uncooperative parents of all the students in her class. Her only involvement in her son's education seemed to be getting really angry and complaining from time to time.

Instead of responding to the mother's complaints with criticism of her own, though, Ms. Garcia said, "So, what do you suggest that we do for Alex? I have some ideas, but I'd like to hear yours first."

The mom said, "Well, you're the teacher. I would hope that you had ideas. But so far they haven't done much good. He got better grades in his other classes before yours, so you must be doing something wrong."

Ms. Garcia believed that Alex's previous teachers had given him higher grades than he should have received, in order to avoid dealing with this mother. It sounds as if all this mom cared about was grades, not what her son was actually learning. But Alex wasn't performing at a higher level and Ms. Garcia was not going to say that he was or just hand out better grades.

Here's how the rest of their conversation played out:

Ms. Garcia, "Well, there are lots of options. Do you want to hear some of them? Or did you have something in mind?"

Alex's mom: "You could make your class more interesting. Then maybe he would pay more attention."

This really irritated Ms. Garcia, because she worked so hard at making her class interesting. But she held her tongue. "Okay," she said. "Any other suggestions?"

Alex's mom: "You could make him pay attention—just get angry at him when you see that he's starting to drift away from what you're talking about."

Ms. Garcia thought to herself that getting angry probably happens a lot at Alex's home and doesn't seem to be helping him. But she calmly asked: "Any more ideas?"

Alex's mom: "No. What are you going to do?"

Ms. Garcia: "Let me tell you what some of our options are. Alex does seem to have some trouble keeping his attention focused on task. Do you notice that at home? You could have him assessed by a doctor. It's up to you. And since I can't spend a lot of time individually with him to focus his attention, you might consider sitting down and asking him questions about what he's learning. This sometimes helps students who are struggling—you can focus his attention by having him sit down, without any other distractions, like TV or eating or anything else. Then just have a four- to five-minute conversation about what he's learning. You could also ask him what his homework is each day when he gets home. If you want, you could write me a note about how the conversation goes and if there's anything you want to tell me about what he says he needs help with."

Alex's mom: "Can I email you?"

Ms. Garcia: "Sure. I'll try to get back to you within 24 hours, if I can. Is that okay with you?"

Mom: "Yeah, that's fine. It feels like we're working together on this."

Ms. Garcia: "Yes, we're working together for Alex's benefit. That's a good thing. Any other issues you want to bring up?"

Mom: "No. That's it for now."

Ms. Garcia: "Great. So I will look for emails from you, and you can focus on discussing what he's learning at school and what his homework is. Something for each of us to do. Thanks for coming in."

Mom: "Thank you."

Discussion of This Example

You can see how Ms. Garcia avoided defending herself and avoided trying to prove how "interesting" her classroom is. She also refrained from attacking or criticizing her student's mother. Instead, she kept the focus on the mom and her various complaints. This way, she was able to manage her better and get a constructive conversation going. By asking for *her suggestions*, she shifted the mom's focus from complaining to potential solutions. By waiting to provide her own ideas until after Alex's mom had offered some, Ms. Garcia was able to avoid being a target for the mom's anger and the mom became absorbed in talking about solutions.

While it may seem surprising that Ms. Garcia invited this mom to send her notes or emails, this teacher knew that writing has a calming effect on high-conflict people—or any anxious person. They know that what they write will receive attention, rather than be ignored or brushed off. That is one of the common complaints of HCPs, and knowing that you will listen makes them less likely to do something dramatic to get your attention.

Another factor in the success of this conversation was that Ms. Garcia emphasized that they were working together for Alex's benefit. By talking about *"our* options," she was able to treat the problem as something that required a team effort, rather than just the mom's problem or the teacher's problem. You might think of this as "building a team against the problem," rather than one person against the other. This seems to help with HCPs, who may automatically think in terms of "me versus you," unless you can build a team approach and draw them in—as Ms. Garcia did.

By asking for proposals (suggestions) and offering proposals (options), the teacher was able to quickly calm the conflict and actually make progress for the benefit of this child.

The High School Student

Vicki and Paul Gable were divorced for three years when their son, Nate, entered tenth grade.

"I want our son to go to college," Paul said to Vicki on the phone. "That's how you get ahead in the world today."

"But you know he's not a very good student," Vicki insisted. "It's too much pressure on him to try to go to college. I think he would do better learning a skill that uses his hands."

"There isn't much money in that," Paul said. "Let's sit down with him and discuss it—see what he's thinking about his future."

"He isn't thinking about his future," Vicki said. "That's part of the problem."

"Tell him we want to jointly have a meeting with him about his future, and we want to know his ideas too," he said. "He lives mostly with you, so you need to be the one to set it up."

Later that day, Vicki approached her son, "Nate, your father and I want to have a meeting with you to start talking about your future."

"I don't want a meeting. Can't you just leave my future up to me?" Nate exclaimed.

"That's not one of the options," Vicki said. "You can't live here for the rest of your life. We need to find a time either this weekend or next weekend. I'll give you 24 hours to propose a day and a couple times, if you want. If you don't by then, we will pick a date and time to meet."

Nate was used to his parents asking him to make proposals. "Oh, all right! How about next Sunday afternoon—around two or four?"

On the next Sunday at 4 p.m. at Vicki's house, Paul explained, "We want the best for you, Nate. We're willing to help you go to college. We have some money saved. But first we need to know what you think about your future."

"I don't know if I want to go to college," Nate replied. "I don't know what I want to do. I'd really like to travel and see the world. I like wild adventures, you know that."

"Yes, we do. You're great at that," said Vicki. Nate was a skilled athlete, especially skateboarding, and he was getting into surfing now, since his mom lived near the beach. "But it takes money. How do you plan to earn the money to do that—to see the world?"

"I'll win some competitions," Nate quickly replied. "I'll earn my own money that way. Until that happens, can I live with one of you guys for a couple extra years? It will really help if I can keep living near the beach until I win some competitions."

"Well, that's one option," Vicki commented, with a skeptical frown. "But it's a very long shot. You know that. There aren't many professional skateboarders or surfers. I'm not sure I would be helping you by letting you live here for free after you graduate high school."

Paul looked at Vicki and said, "That wouldn't be a good idea. It will set him back if you let him get away with that. That's the opposite of what he needs." Turning to Nate, "Do you have any other ideas? We're not going to be around forever to support you, like we do now. You'll have a lot more choices if you go to college."

"Yeah, but they say that college doesn't make a difference anymore," Nate said. "You can learn everything on the Internet now. Look at Mark Zuckerberg and Bill Gates—they both dropped out of college. Look at them!"

"But they both got into Harvard," Paul retorted. "If you can get into Harvard, you're going to have a pretty good future regardless of what you do. But do you have any research to support your point of view—that college graduates don't make any more than high school graduates nowadays?"

"No, but everyone knows it. The world has changed!"

"Not that much," said his mother.

"Tell you what," Paul interrupted. "I will support you living at home—either one of our homes—for four years after you graduate high school *if* you can show me credible proof that having a college degree wouldn't make a difference financially for your future. What do you think about that idea? And if you can't find such proof, then will you agree to tell us three colleges you might want to go to? Or some other career path that you want us to help you with? You need to come up with some proposals—unless you can find evidence that college doesn't matter anymore."

"Don't push him too hard, Paul. He's still in high school," Vicki said.

"Well, we're trying to save up to help him with college. He needs to start thinking about it too."

"Okay, okay!" Nate exclaimed. "I'll come up with something. Can I go now?"

"All right," Paul replied. "We'll give you a couple weeks to think about this and come up with a few proposals for how we can help you with your career choices. And let me know what you find out about whether college doesn't matter anymore."

Two weeks later, Nate talked to his parents. "Okay, Dad. You were right. A two-year college program gets you 22 percent more income than high school, and a four-year college gets you 66 percent more. It actually got me thinking about going into some kind of sports medicine—you know, physical therapy or maybe even being a doctor. I realize I've got to get my grades up these next couple years. Will you guys help me figure out where I can afford to go? I'll need to apply next year."

"I really like your proposals, Nate," Paul said.

"Oh, they're not proposals. That's what I've decided," said Nate, emphatically.

"Well, great!" his father exclaimed. "Let us know how we can help. And we'll let you know what we can afford. Right, Vicki?"

"Right! For sure. Good choice. You've really surprised me and I'll do what I can to help. Remember, we love you no matter which choices you make."

Discussion of This Example

Paul and Vicki got Nate thinking about his choices by telling him what they were willing to do and asking him what he proposed—or at least was thinking—about his future. Although Paul was intending to be rigid about Nate attending college, he started to look at it as just one option among many. Vicki was going to be rigid about not putting too much pressure on Nate. But by approaching the discussion as one about choices for them and choices for Nate, they got Nate *thinking* with his problem-solving brain without getting stuck in his defensive brain—which would have happened had his parents started arguing about his future.

Since a major aspect of the teenage years is learning how to think through problems, educating a teenager about choices and encouraging him or her to make proposals based on those choices is essential. Brain scientists say that the brain isn't fully developed until about age twenty-five. Much of the later stages of this development occurs in the prefrontal cortex, the area of the brain where we learn to override impulsive and overreactive emotions and behavior. It helps if parents can work together on helping their teen learn to make decisions, especially because at least half of teenagers today have parents who are separated or divorced.

It also helps to predict setbacks and allow high school students to experience failures and then get back on their feet again. If Nate does or doesn't get his grades up, it will help him make decisions about his career. His parents understand that his recent "decision" isn't really final, but they don't want to discourage him. High school students are supposed to be getting ready to be adults by experimenting with different friends, behaviors, styles, interests— and by overcoming failures, so that they learn how to handle failures later on as adults.

Some parents try to protect their children from setbacks, but in so doing their kids never learn the skills they need to move forward and overcome setbacks as adults. Children who grow up feeling entitled to success have a much harder time as adults, because they can't cope with failures. Many high-conflict people have this characteristic of becoming enraged when they fail at something. It's better to learn how to overcome obstacles while you're young and have more support and information available from family members, friends, teachers, and others.

College and Graduate School

College students and graduate students are learning what their interests are and how good they are at different skills. Since they will live and work in a world that will be quite different from today, they need to develop flexible thinking about their careers. Some of the most important skills for them to learn include how to gather relevant information, make reasonable proposals, respond to the proposals of others, and, finally, make decisions. Therefore, it will be important for their parents, teachers, and administrators to help them learn these skills, rather than to make decisions for them—to the full extent possible.

In the past, teachers and parents would back each other up when it came to children's academic and behavior problems. But today, everything is expected to be negotiable; therefore, expectations and responsibilities are unclear and parents and teachers are often in conflict. Given the increase in high-conflict people in the world, it's no surprise that some of them end up at school—as students, as parents, and sometimes as teachers.

Children's anxiety tends to reflect and feed off the anxiety of their parents. The term "helicopter parent" didn't exist in popular culture until the beginning of this century, but today we recognize that some parents do indeed hover over their children, as if to control and/or protect them at any moment. At a seminar I was conducting at a university a few years ago, a professor told the story of one such parent:

> After class, one of my students in his early twenties came up to me and said, "My mother is angry that you gave me a 'B' in the exam and she wants to talk to you!" Then, he handed me his cell phone with his mother on the line, who wanted to somehow negotiate his grade for him.

At first, teachers and administrators in higher education tried to get parents to leave their young adult children alone to deal with their own successes and failures. However, nowadays, teachers and administrators realize that parents are going to be involved whether they like it or not, so the only question is how to make it a positive involvement. One approach is to involve them in meetings about the student's academics or behavior.

The College Student

Jonathan, age 20, is an undergraduate student in a health sciences program who is doing quite poorly, nearly failing his courses. His parents are outraged that the department is considering kicking him out of the program. At least one faculty member also suspects that he may be cheating on tests, although this is hard to prove.

Dr. Alice Almar is the college's assistant dean in charge of meeting with students about academic dismissals and conduct issues. Jonathan's parents requested to sit in on the meeting with Dr. Almar and their son.

In years gone by, such a meeting would have been an

important point in an adult student's learning process. Facing severe consequences can be motivating *toward* a career or *away* from a career. Perhaps a student like Jonathon will work harder or decide that this is not the field for him.

Therefore, it is a complicating factor when parents intervene in a young adult's educational choices. Still, many universities have decided to engage the parents, rather than try to keep them out, when difficult decisions need to be made and the parents insist on being involved. Their interest and involvement is not completely unreasonable—after all, many of them are paying the tuition bills. Plus, many of them will become heavily involved in their student's career options and housing plans if the student is excused from the university.

"Thank you for meeting with me, Jonathan. And I'm pleased to meet both of you today," Dr. Almar said, introducing herself to Jonathan's parents. "I'm glad you could join us for today's important meeting. Please be seated and be comfortable," said Dr. Almar.

"You need to know how concerned we are about Jonathan's future!" his mother immediately went on the offensive, while his father nodded his head in agreement. "We are concerned that this university has not been giving our son the support he needs. We understand that he may have fallen a little behind, but we don't understand why the teachers are not doing more to help him. We pay a lot in tuition to this school. Why are we now hearing that he may be failing out of the program?"

"I appreciate your concern," Dr. Almar said. "I know this is an important time for all of you. We all have the same goal: to create a plan for which Jonathan can be successful, with a match to his future academic and career goals. We are facing some big decisions. Do you want to know how Jonathan is doing first? Or hear what some of our options are at this point?"

"Jonathan?" his mother said, angrily turning to her son.

"I know I'm having a hard time," started Jonathan. "I thought

I was better at chemistry and biology than I seem to be. I'm enjoying my part-time job as a nurse's aide—maybe I just like the people part more than the science part."

His father chimed in: "There's not much of a future in being a nurse's aide." Then, turning to Dr. Almar, he said, "Don't you have something better for my son to do here? He was an 'A' student in high school."

Dr. Almar suspects that Jonathan was spending a lot of time with a new girlfriend and not studying as much as he needed to. But she was avoiding going there in front of his parents.

"Let's look at some scenarios to see how Jonathan can move ahead," Dr. Almar intervened. "It will be up to Jonathon which option he decides on, but I know it is important to consider your input. We meet with a lot of parents and expect that they will be advocates for their sons and daughters."

"Yes, tell us!" his mother demanded.

"When a student is struggling in this many classes, we offer the student the option of taking off a semester or two, to get some tutoring, clear his head, rethink his career options, perhaps try a temporary job in another field," explained Dr. Almar. "Another option is to leave the university altogether and plan to start over somewhere else—perhaps taking a year off from school. A third option is to continue his enrollment here and try to focus more on the courses he is having trouble in. As it stands, he is on probation and if he continues on this course, he will have an official dismissal on his transcript. This could leave us no better off than today but with another semester of tuition costs.

"There is another very serious issue to consider," Dr. Almar continued. "It has been brought to the department chair's attention that Jonathan is under a high level of suspicion for breaking the academic honesty rules. The full investigation needs to take place, and it is not appropriate or productive to adjudicate this now. What is important is to put on this table any barriers or concerns that we have. Jonathan, let's start with how you are spending your days."

"Did you cheat, honey!" demanded Jonathon's mother.

"No, of course not!" Jonathan replied in disgust. "I would never cheat on an exam! You know that!"

"He's never failed at anything before," his father jumped in. "I won't have him being seen as a failure."

"Well," Dr. Almar responded calmly, "people learn a lot about themselves and their interests when they fail at something. Some very well-known people failed at what they thought they would be good at. For example, Mahatma Ghandi failed the bar exam twice after he got out of law school. So he left India and went to South Africa for many years and learned to become a political leader. Then, he returned to India and changed the course of history. If he had passed the bar the first or second time, we probably would never have heard of him. Thomas Jefferson was a failure at being a governor. Jane Addams thought she wanted to be a doctor but ended up helping more people as a pioneer in acclimating immigrants to the big city."

"I didn't know any of that," Jonathon's father exclaimed.

"Do you have any questions, Jonathan?" Dr. Almar asked. "What do you propose, given the options we discussed or any others you can think of?"

"I propose that I wait a couple weeks and think about it. Can I do that?"

"Sure. Taking the time to think it through is best. Get back to me before two weeks though, because we're up against the deadlines for registration for next semester's classes. As you know, the academic calendar moves on . . ."

"That's the choice I want to make right now. Is that okay with you, Mom and Dad?"

Turning to his parents, Dr. Almar said, "We are glad that you chose our school. Jonathan's grades in high school were very good, and you had other choices. But now we need to understand the best way to move forward to meet Jonathon's academic and career goals. We want to come up with the best plan where he will continue to have success."

"Thank you," his mother said and smiled. "Thanks for being patient with us. I think you can understand how much we have high hopes for Jonathan and this is quite a setback for us."

"I can understand that. But your son has options and a lot of that is thanks to both of you for supporting him. Do you have any other questions for me?" Dr. Almar asked.

"No. Thanks again," his father said. They all shook hands on their way out of the office.

Discussion of This Example

Dr. Almar kept the emphasis on choices for Jonathan and his parents. She didn't argue with them and calmed them with her problem-solving approach. She avoided criticizing Jonathan in front of his parents, yet got her points across about the decisions that would need to be made about his future. Jonathon and his parents left the meeting knowing that the outcome would be up to him—or them—rather than the school deciding it all for him.

If Dr. Almar had made the decision for him/them, and if one or more of them were high-conflict people, then they would have put all of their energy into fighting against that decision—and possibly making a great deal of trouble for the university. After all, I am told that about 10 percent of the students take up about 90 percent of the assistant dean's time at many universities. But when the decision-making responsibility is set on the student's and parents' shoulders, they are more likely to really think the issues through and to accept whatever he/they decide.

Summary

Education is an area ripe for high-conflict behavior: people have high expectations, they feel very vulnerable, and disappointments are bound to occur. What's more, the types and ages of various people in this setting are prone to defensive reactions. First, students under twenty-five are still experiencing brain development, and so they have less impulse control, judgment, and experience with responsibility, making defensive reacting more common for them. Second, today's parents are more involved in their children's education than ever before, and a higher percentage have high-conflict personalities than in the past. And, finally, some teachers and administrators have high-conflict personalities themselves; they are attracted to working with students because they enjoy dominating others and being looked up to as a way to manage their own distress. Fortunately, this is a small percentage, though is probably growing as well.

With all of this said, however, when conflict occurs, it can help to emphasize that everyone has choices and to offer options and ask for proposals. This keeps responsibility on the shoulders of everyone, including potential HCPs, who try to blame others for their own behavior. By using this general approach, it is possible to manage difficult people and also to consistently teach responsibility at a vulnerable age throughout an educational institution or setting.

CHAPTER SEVEN

Consequences in Families

High-conflict people tend to be focused on the present, with little thought about the future consequences of their actions. This may be because a lot of HCPs were physically abused growing up. When they were bad, they got hit; and when they were good, they got hit. They learned that it didn't much matter what they did, because their own behavior had little influence on what happened to them.

Nowadays, we also see a lot of HCPs who were entitled as children. When they were good, they got what they wanted. When they were bad, they got what they wanted. So they, too, don't seem to think as much about the consequences of their actions. It didn't really matter what they did—the results were the same.

In addition to these trends, many parents today try to protect their children from the negative consequences of their actions by being the "helicopter parents" described in the previous chapter. As a result, their children don't get much practice at thinking ahead; instead, they stay focused on what they want in the present moment or react to their current life circumstances considering the future.

With this characteristic of HCPs in mind, it is particularly important for parents and professionals to explain the consequences of a child's actions, to help the child think about his or her own behavior. It is also necessary to take this approach with adults who have become HCPs. A lot of people do not realize that HCPs aren't thinking about the consequences; they often just assume HCPs are purposefully acting badly "with full knowledge of the consequences." It helps to learn that this is not the case. They are acting *without thinking* about the effects. Therefore, it can help to educate them about the consequences that they may not know or to remind them to consider the consequences that they do know but have forgotten about in the intensity of their current emotions.

This chapter focuses on the consequences of behavior in families, but the concepts we'll discuss can be applied in any setting.

Today's Relationship Behavior Has Consequences

Family relationships and close friendships involve choices and consequences. Traditionally, family roles and rules were clear-cut and structured in a top-down manner, and everyone knew who was in charge of what (Dad—job; Mom—kids and house; older kids—younger kids). Relationships were secure no matter how you behaved. You acted badly, you got punished—but you were still part of the family.

Today, most family relationships are voluntary after the first few years of childhood. That is, people choose to be together or choose to leave the relationship. Approximately half of marriages end in divorce. Adult children move away to other states, and some break off all contact with one or both parents. Teenagers spend more time with their friends (or texting them) than with their parents—even when they're physically in the same room. Young children average several hours a day watching television and playing on their devices, often learning lessons for life that are the opposite of what their parents are teaching them—such as have minimal empathy or respect for others, you can't trust anyone, or people are worthless unless they're rich and famous—all of which undermine healthy family relationships.

In these ways, family relationships are more uncertain in today's world and mostly negotiable. One of the key new skills that everyone needs to learn, therefore, is how to routinely make proposals instead of demands; how to respectfully consider the proposals of others; and how to make decisions that will not threaten the relationship but help strengthen it.

High-Conflict People in Families

Dealing with ordinary relationship changes and stressors in families is made even more challenging when high-conflict people are involved, because they frequently act in a manner that would blow up most ordinary relationships—without even realizing it—until people abandon them or emotionally leave the relationship.

Expressing intense anger or remaining silent for hours or days on end are common behaviors with HCPs. They may make threats (of violence, property damage, walking out, spreading rumors, showing up at your work, etc.) to keep the other person "in line." Yet all of these methods and tactics common to HCPs are also effective ways to blow up a relationship.

HCPs don't understand this. How could this happen? They seem to lack the empathy and self-awareness to see the role they played in pushing people away from them. Those involved in high-conflict divorces spend years in family courts playing out HCP anger over the loss of a love relationship. Ironically, many of the angry HCPs engage in this behavior in an effort to get their loved one back into the relationship. Not surprisingly, their escalating anger backfires and pushes people farther away.

Teaching Children about Consequences

Children today need to learn about the consequences of their relationship behavior more than in the past, rather than less. Yet, today's children are more often protected from the consequences of their actions by well-intentioned parents, grandparents, and others. This leads to unrealistic expectations for their future relationships, which will be voluntary and with people who are less tolerant than their parents and other family members. This may be one of several contributing factors to the recent increase in young adults with personality disorders.

Therefore, it will become more and more important to teach children to manage relationships by regularly making proposals, rather than making demands or giving up, and for parents to demonstrate this approach in their own relationships.

This chapter provides examples of ways to teach an out-of-control child about consequences and choices and consequences when a couple is facing divorce.

Moderate Emotional Range

Family relationships and close friendships need to operate in what would be defined as a "moderate emotional range" to survive. That is, there needs to be enough emotional energy to keep the parties from drifting apart but not so much energy that it blows up the relationship. Since HCPs routinely feel weak, vulnerable, and helpless, they often shift to extreme behavior to feel strong—but at the same time they push away the people closest to them.

It's important, then, for adults and children to learn how to negotiate their relationships, so they can avoid losing them. But how do you teach this to children—and especially young teenagers—who feel such intense new emotions that blame and rage may become common? Some may become HCPs if these behaviors turn into habits and become embedded in their personalities. The key to helping them develop negotiation skills is in laying the groundwork before problems get started or getting help if a teenager gets stuck in this behavior. (Note: All parents should also prepare to manage sudden outbursts of blame and anger.)

Does Mark Hate His Mom?

Mark was big for a thirteen-year-old. In fact, he was bigger than his petite mother, Patti. They were about the same height, but Mark had grown a lot heavier. His parents got divorced when Mark was eleven, although they were still generally friendly and supportive of each other. Because of his busy work schedule, Mark's father, Roger, agreed that his son should live primarily with Patti. Mark blamed Patti for breaking up the family and as he grew taller and heavier, he started hitting his mother—playfully at first. But Patti was intimidated, partly because of the boy's size and partly because she felt guilty about the divorce, which had been her idea. So she tolerated being hit by her growing son and did not impose any negative consequences for this behavior. After all, she knew he was having a hard time coping with the divorce and becoming an adolescent who was the wrong size compared to many of his classmates.

She would say, "Stop it!" But he would back off and then playfully hit her again.

He would say, "You can't make me stop it." And Patti knew that he was right.

Finally, Patti told Roger that this was becoming a problem—a serious problem. "What do you propose? I'm at my wit's end," she told him. "If this is what he's doing to me at thirteen, I may not survive his teenage years. I'm getting really scared of him."

"I have no idea what to do," Roger said. "But I don't want this to continue. Can't you just firmly set limits with him? Tell him you'll take away his cell phone or ground him for the weekend?"

"The problem is that he spends most of the weekend at home in his room. He won't even let me come in. When I give him a hard time, he threatens to hit me. Then he says he'd rather live with you full-time anyway. He thinks the worst that could happen is that you would let him live with you. It's like I have no power over him at all. It's easier just to leave him alone in there."

"All right, let's talk to a counselor," Roger said, frustrated.

After talking on the phone with a counselor who worked with children and families, Roger and Patti agreed to meet with the counselor in person before bringing in their son.

"Can you get him to stop hitting his mother—just by talking to him?" asked Roger.

"No," Ms. Sorda replied. "It's going to take both of you, plus me—and possibly a treatment center. From what you are describing, this behavior has been going on for at least a couple of years, in one form or another. It's going to take intensive treatment to shift him from assaulting you to treating you with respect. It's becoming part of who he is."

"Yes, and he's starting to get in fights at school, too. Would it help for him to move in with his father?" Patti asked, looking at Roger.

"But I don't want to give him what he wants—to reward him for his bad behavior. I don't think that's a good solution. Plus, I'm not always around; I'm out of town from time to time these days."

"Perhaps he doesn't realize that living with you is not an option—not one of his choices," Ms. Sorda said. "I suggest that we three have a session with Mark and let him know what his choices really are. We also need to talk about what the consequences of his actions are going to be and explain that he is making a choice with his behavior."

"Will you tell him that?" Patti suggested, eagerly.

"No, I think it has to come from you two. But I can help you do this. First, I need to know if you are willing to send him to a treatment center if he chooses to keep hitting you. You will have to be very firm and very united in making this decision. What do you think?"

"I'm not sure that we could afford this," Roger replied. "I'll have to check out my insurance and see if it covers treatment centers like you're describing."

"Keep in mind that you may not be able to afford to let this problem continue, either," Ms. Sorda said, raising an eyebrow.

"I just know that I need both of your help," Patti added. "Tell me what to do."

They scheduled a family counseling session, and Patti told Mark he needed to attend with her and his father.

"I won't go," Mark said.

Patti, feeling encouraged by Ms. Sorda, raised her voice for the first time in a long time and said, "Yes, you will! If you want to live in my house, you will go with me to see this counselor."

"I don't care if I live in your house. I'll just go live with Dad."

"Your father supports me in this. He's going to be there too."

"I don't believe you," Mark sassed back. "Call him."

Patti angrily replied, "I will call him and you'll see what he says. He agrees with me."

"Then you shouldn't have divorced him," Mark sassed back again.

On the phone with his father, Mark said, "I want to come live with you. Mom's a real pain in the butt."

"We can talk about that at this meeting with the counselor," his father said calmly, as he had been advised to do if this issue came up.

At the family session, Ms. Sorda explained that everyone has to live with choices and consequences in their lives.

"I want to live with my father!" Mark interrupted. "I don't need any counseling. This is all my mother's problem—she constantly bugs me. If she would only leave me alone, everything would be fine. She's the one who needs counseling."

"Actually, I am going to get some counseling," his mother chimed in. "But that's not why we're here today. We need to talk about your choices and consequences."

"Dad, just tell them I can live with you and we'll be all done."

"Mark, you can't speak to me or your mother this way. First, you need to listen to Ms. Sorda; then I'll tell you my choice."

"What do you mean, your choice, Dad?"

"Listen to Ms. Sorda; then we'll talk about it."

Ms. Sorda said, "A big part of learning for all of us, especially in our teenage years, is how to get along in relationships. What you learn now will help you or hurt you for the rest of your life. You're actions are helping wire your brain for solutions that you will use automatically throughout your adult life. If you're learning to hit your mother as the way to get what you think you want, then you will probably do this with your girlfriends and your wife. That can get you into a lot of trouble—you could even go to jail. That's the adult consequence of domestic violence. And hitting anyone in the family is domestic violence.

"So now is the best time to learn different ways of solving problems," the counselor continued. "You need to practice talking and listening respectfully to people, while also sticking up for yourself. So I have recommended that you participate in a discussion group that I run for teenagers who have trouble saying what they're feeling and wanting, and who need more practice."

"I'm not gonna do that!" Mark said, frowning at his parents.

"Well, that's what I'm recommending," Ms. Sorda said. "But I know the decision is up to your parents. Keep in mind that it's your inappropriate behavior that caused us to have this meeting. If you were acting appropriately at home, we wouldn't be sitting here right now. This is one of the consequences of your behavior. Of course, if you suddenly started behaving appropriately, it might be a sign that you don't need such a group. But it might be easier to just participate in the group and learn some new ways of talking respectfully to people and expressing your needs. Perhaps your behavior over the next two to three weeks will tell us which option you prefer. That is, if you parents want to give you a choice at all."

Ms. Sorda turned to Mark's parents and asked, "Do you want to tell Mark what his options and consequences are at this point?"

Roger spoke up: "You have asked to live with me, but I have decided that's not one of your choices at this time. I'm not around enough and your behavior should not be rewarded by giving in to what you want after you have behaved so badly. It's a disservice to your mother and to your future. So if you can't live with your mother, you will need to live in a treatment center for a while. Here are your choices: Live with your mother and treat her with respect, and never hit her again. Or go to a treatment center to learn how to behave in relationships with anyone. Now your mother has something to tell you."

"Yes," Patti joined in. "Your father and I agree that you have two choices and that your choices have consequences. You can choose to live with me respectfully, or you can choose to live at the treatment center. If you choose to live with me, then I will expect you to attend Ms. Sorda's discussion group once a week. It's with teenagers like you who are having some trouble but are willing to learn. If you say you want to live with me, we will see if your behavior matches that choice. If your behavior indicates to me that you are choosing to live at the treatment center for a while, then that will be arranged. So, you see, it's up to you!"

"I don't need a treatment center—" Mark shouted.

"Mark," Ms. Sorda interrupted. "If you're going to use words, you'll have more success if you say, 'I don't think I need a treatment center. I want to try to make it work at home with you, Mom.' Or something like that."

"Yeah," Mark tried to calm himself, quietly saying, "That's what I want—what she said."

"Can you say it, Mark?" Patti asked, feeling much stronger.

Straightening in his chair, Mark said, "I'll try to be good, Mom. I really will. I'm sorry." He had a tear in his eye.

At that moment his mother had a flash of insight: *He's just a big baby who doesn't know what to do.* And she came over and gave him a hug, which he accepted. His father came over and gave him a hug too.

Ms. Sorda, having witnessed such moments many times before, said, "Now don't think this is the end of it all. This is just the beginning. It's your choice—all of you—on a daily basis. Don't forget that you're all going to need to make some changes for this to work out. That's why we have a group at our clinic for parents of teenagers as well. I hope you parents will attend that. It can make a world of difference for all of you."

Discussion of This Example

This case demonstrates several ideas related to proposals, choices, and consequences. First, here was a "child" who had gotten used to some bad relationship behavior that could haunt him his whole life if he didn't change it. Of course, it's easier to alter behavior at age 13—when the brain is still rapidly changing and developing—than at 23 or 33. And while change is certainly still possible for adults, it is harder.

Mark's story also demonstrates a negative consequence for the parents from allowing their son's behavior to continue without consequences for so long. The consequence was that Patti felt more and more intimidated in her own home. While we hear a lot in the news about domestic violence by husbands and boyfriends (and some wives and girlfriends), there's little public discussion of abuse involving children who hit their parents—and children who hate their parents. Such acting out is often the accumulative effect of tolerating bad relationship behavior for years—behavior that needed to be confronted when it started, not two years later.

This problem of children and teens with out-of-control behavior also poses negative consequences for society. Over the past 20 years, treatment centers, such as the one described in Mark's case, have had funding reduced at the same time that more and more children appear to be having mental health problems. Some reports indicate that 25 percent of today's teens have experienced a diagnosable mental health problem, a rate higher than in previous generations. The consequence of cutting funding for youth and mental health needs can impact society as a whole, as we have seen with recent incidents of public violence by young adults with serious mental health problems.

On the positive side, Mark's parents took action to educate themselves and their son about choices and consequences. In the real case this story is based on, the teen did end up in a residential treatment center for a few months before his new behavior became consistent enough for him to eventually move back in with his mother—without violence and other negativity. And this positive outcome came about because these divorced parents started working together on addressing Mark's problems; they got help, rather than fighting with each other. The positive consequence of a positive choice.

And Mark didn't hate his mother. He just had a behavior problem that needed to be managed—with choices and consequences.

Making a List in Couples Counseling

Kamal and Mani had been married for 25 years when they came in for couples' counseling. Kamal, the wife, wanted to end the marriage. It had been an arranged marriage in their home country when she was 13 and he was 26. She had raised six children while Mani had built a very successful career as a software engineer and worked his way into upper management in his company.

But Mani seemed to love Kamal and was willing to do almost anything to make her happy in the marriage. They had two homes, and he was willing to remodel them, buy a new home, or do whatever else it took to satisfy his wife. She seemed intense, thought their counselor, Mr. Windham. Kamal said that she still loved Mani but that she needed to create her own life now. She felt suffocated in the marriage and abandoned by Mani to his work. She had never been on her own and was exhausted from family life, when it seemed like there was so much opportunity for her, too, in the United States.

After getting some history of the marriage and the couple's goals, Mr. Windham encouraged them to agree to at least eight sessions of couples' counseling before making any final decisions about their marriage. This was because the first two to three sessions may feel uncomfortable as they open up subjects they hadn't talked about for years. Kamal and Mani both agreed to wait on any decision making for eight weeks.

During the sessions, Mr. Windham noticed that Kamal seemed to be quite dramatic, almost histrionic, and saw things in terms of all-or-nothing solutions while Mani seemed more self-absorbed. The therapist wondered if getting divorced was another extreme solution for Kamal, or if Mani would be relieved to have less of a roller coaster in his life. They seemed to be a potentially high-conflict couple headed for divorce. But he would do the best he could while they agreed to come.

For homework after their third session, Mr. Windham suggested that they each make two lists: (1) a list of what they would need to do and decide if they split up; and (2) a list of what they would each need to do to make the relationship work better if they stayed together. He told them not to discuss or share their lists until they met with him again.

When they read their lists at the next session, Kamal said, "One of the big things I want is to go to college. I always wanted to do that and you would never let me go."

"I never said that," Mani replied. "If you want to go to college, you should do that. You have my full support."

"I do?" Kamal exclaimed in surprise. "You always said I needed to stay home with the children, that home is where I belonged."

"No," Mani insisted. "I even said you could work if you wanted to. I just thought that you would want to stay home with the children. They were your life, you said."

"Well, of course the children were and are my life. But I want to make more of my life now that they're almost all grown up. Are you saying you would allow me to go to college now?"

"Absolutely! Why didn't you say that before?"

"I didn't realize this until I wrote my list. I guess I totally believed that it was out of the question for you—that you wanted me at home, like so many of the women in our family traditionally have done."

"That was in your head," Mani replied. "It didn't come from me. If you had brought it up, I would have said yes."

"Then I guess we're done here," Kamal said excitedly, turning to Mr. Windham. "That's all I needed to know. I'm willing to give this marriage another chance, if I can develop myself now."

"That's great," Mr. Windham said. "Stopping now is one

option. But I would suggest that we finish out the eight sessions, so that any other misunderstandings can get resolved and you can have skills for negotiating future conflicts—without having to go to the extreme of considering divorce if there are disagreements."

"What do you want to do?" Kamal looked at Mani.

"I want to do what you want to do," Mani said. "I don't want us to talk about getting divorced when there's trouble. I think we can solve things if you just speak up about what you want, instead of blaming me for the past."

"I want to stop the counseling now, since we've solved this," she said. "We've finished what we've come here for."

"It's up to both of you," Mr. Windham said. "You know what I think is best—to focus on learning skills now, especially when you have such a good start, so that you don't get to this point again. That's why I suggested at the start that you both commit to at least eight sessions. It's not unusual that people resolve one issue but then get stuck on another. But you can feel free to call me at any time and set something up. In the meantime, you can always make a list of proposals or requests of each other at any time. It's up to both of you."

They decided to stop the counseling and Mr. Windham never saw them again. Good news? It's always hard to tell. Many couples on the verge of divorce are able to stay married and make it work sufficiently. Many other couples end up solving one problem but then get overwhelmed and end up pursuing a divorce six to twelve months later. Learning skills—especially relationship negotiation skills—can make a huge difference, as they are usually easier to learn *before* problems get so big that people are seriously considering divorce.

Discussion of This Example

Was Kamal or Mani a high-conflict person? It's always hard to know after meeting with them so briefly. But the idea of making a list of options or proposals can help any couple or other people in a conflict. It shifts the focus away from blame and the past and onto what to do now. It seemed that Kamal had some traits of a dramatic, all-or-nothing personality and this structured approach helped her think more effectively. Of course, she also applied an all-or-nothing approach to the counseling—once she got something big she wanted, she quickly left behind the idea of learning skills to solve future problems. This demonstrates the potentially self-defeating aspects of this all-or-nothing characteristic of HCPs.

In terms of consequences, Mr. Windham did inform the couple that they just might get divorced later on if they didn't sufficiently learn skills now for negotiating in relationships. But he emphasized that there was a choice—that it was up to them (*both* of them) to decide, which strengthens the "team against the problem" approach instead of one against the other. The counselor also made certain that he stressed this point to both of them, because Mani seemed more reasonable and more likely to look at consequences in making decisions. Of course, Mani didn't seem to want to challenge Kamal when she was happy with him.

By emphasizing that the decision was up to them, Mr. Windham operated on the idea that trying to coerce a potential HCP usually backfires, which is why he didn't put too much emphasis on their prior agreement to attend eight sessions. Demanding that HCPs do what *you think* they should do is almost guaranteed to inspire them to do the opposite. That's why it is so effective to make proposals, lists, requests, options, and choices when negotiating with HCPs. Even if they don't do what you think they should do, you can walk away from the relationship without turning it into an unnecessary crisis with intense blame and possibly extreme behavior against you.

For example, any professionals who aren't careful in their work with HCPs and their families risk being sued or having a licensing action brought against them when HCP clients feel abandoned, disrespected, dominated, threatened, or ignored. And nowadays we increasingly see HCP family members suing other family members for the same reasons. But educating them about the consequences of their decisions and actions can make a difference—it can get them thinking instead of just reacting.

Summary

This chapter has demonstrated how choices and consequences go together, especially in family relationships or any ongoing relationship. Each individual's choices can influence the future or the end of the relationship. High-conflict people tend to be preoccupied with the present and aren't usually thinking about the consequences of their actions. Yet in families today, high-conflict behavior can lead to the end of the relationship.

High-conflict people truly want good relationships, but they don't connect their behavior today to what happens to their relationships in the future. Therefore, it's often helpful to calmly explain and repeat the consequences. Making proposals, including writing lists, can help family members slow down and consider each other's needs when making decisions that can have far-reaching effects in the most important relationships in their lives.

CHAPTER EIGHT

Realistic Options in Communities

After our families, our communities can be a source of our greatest pleasure or our worst nightmares. And because more and more people today are discovering that an HCP lives next door or down the street, it's critical to be informed of your realistic options when dealing with a possible HCP in your community. The examples in this chapter demonstrate that importance. The temptation to confront or fight with an HCP may be strong, but these options are unrealistic ways to solve problems when people live very close together. In both of the first two cases presented, no one was surprised at the outcome. In other words, the neighborhood knew there was an HCP around who might take extreme, unpredictable action when he was upset. The third case demonstrates how making and asking for proposals can be effective with a possible HCP neighbor.

The Dogs

A 56-year-old pharmacist was "angry and depressed" when he moved into a townhouse in Phoenix, Arizona. Over the course of a year and a half, he was angry at the barking dogs in the building complex and posted notes on neighbors' doors expressing this anger. He was also having trouble keeping a job. His ex-wife, a behavioral health nurse, later said that he had "depression, paranoia, and self-esteem issues."

One Saturday in 2013, he went to a neighboring townhouse and shot and killed four members of the family inside as well as their two dogs. He then went home and killed himself. His ex-wife said that she "wasn't surprised" when she heard the news. She said the victims were unfortunately in the "wrong place at the wrong time" and "argued with the wrong person."

I don't know any other details of what occurred, but the description of the man's psychological problems and the fact that his ex-wife was not surprised to hear he killed his neighbors suggest that he may have had a high-conflict personality. If the neighbors had understood this, they might have taken a different approach rather than arguing with him. Perhaps they would have discussed proposals—his and theirs—for solving the problems about the dogs' barking. Or maybe they would have proposed that they all go to a mediator or someone else in the community to help them resolve the conflict.

Maybe the dogs' barking wasn't really a problem and it was all in his head, or maybe it was a real nuisance. Either way, respectfully asking, "So, what do you propose?" or suggesting some solutions themselves may have reduced the tension. Often just giving HCPs some respect and taking them seriously helps them calm down.

The Party

Over the course of ten years, one neighbor (Robert Reed) in the generally peaceful neighborhood of Poway outside San Diego, California, seemed in conflict with everyone around him. Neighbors reported that he demanded they not park in front of his house (a public city street) and that he "would become irate if someone tried to turn a car around in his driveway." They learned to "steer clear" of him.

However, in 2008, he was driving around a corner and "swerved as if to hit" another neighbor's son, David Cunnyngham. According to a newspaper report, David Cunnyngham "followed Reed to his house, where they argued." Reed pulled out a small knife and stabbed Cunnyngham twice in the leg. Cunnyngham responded by getting a toolbox out of his truck and hitting Reed in the head with it. Sheriff's deputies came and arrested Reed. However, charges were dropped because of conflicting evidence. Reed's lawyer argued that Cunnyngham started the fight and that

Reed merely pulled out the knife to defend himself. At the time, Cunnyngham's father, Mitch, told the district attorney that Reed "would one day kill someone."

That day came in 2010, when Mitch Cunnyngham and his wife had three other family members over for a barbecue. For some unknown reason, Reed ran down the street to their house (three houses from his) with a shotgun and a handgun. He fired shots into the house and killed Mitch Cunnyngham and his wife. When the sheriff's deputies came, Reed pointed his shotgun at them and refused to put it down, so "both deputies shot and killed him."

Once again, this neighbor may have been an HCP, in which case confronting and challenging him is not the best option for resolving a conflict. HCPs carry resentments and grudges, and it's hard to know if or when they will "snap." When you live in the same neighborhood, frequent contacts can really simmer. It's best to treat such people with respect and a friendly manner, even though you may despise or fear them.

After this incident, the local newspaper included a list of recommendations for "Solving Disputes with Your Neighbors." One was: "Talking to your neighbor in a pleasant way may be all that is needed to work it out." Another was: "When talking doesn't work, a clear written description of the problem *and a proposed solution* may persuade your neighbor" (emphasis added). And of course: "Try mediation."

All of these suggestions fit with the approach of emphasizing proposals rather than demands, whether or not you believe the person is an HCP. But with an HCP, it is essential to avoid demands and direct confrontations. These just escalate the person's defensive-reacting brain and leave problem solving out of reach. For some reason, whatever it is, some HCPs will snap when the average person might not see a problem at all.

I'm not suggesting that neighbors tolerate extreme behavior, but rather that neighbors think through their realistic options when dealing with high-conflict personalities. They may need to set realistic limits on the HCP. Other realistic options for resolving their conflicts may include talking with police or going to mediation, or simply being friendly and not engaging with the person at all. Or it might involve all of the above approaches, as in the following example.

The Owner Next Door

When her parents passed away, Judi inherited and moved into the modest duplex side-by-side home where they had lived for many decades. Although her parents had always rented out the adjacent unit, Judi decided to sell it after she lost her job during the recession of 2008. She needed extra money and decided she could turn her home into two independent units as condominiums. By selling the other unit, she would have a nice chunk of cash she could live on; plus, she would no longer have to deal with the unpredictability of tenants moving in and out, and having an empty unit next door sometimes for months at a time.

After completing all the paperwork to convert the duplex into two condos, she started advertising for a buyer. While several people were interested, she particularly liked a friendly single woman, Trina, who could pay the asking price and who had a sweet ten-year-old daughter. Trina worked from home about ten hours a week giving piano lessons, and she promised to only do that during the daytime. She also said she would put in some soundproofing as she fixed up her place. An extra benefit was that she liked gardening and was interested in working in the yard they shared in the back.

Once the sale was completed and she closed escrow, Trina started making the place her own. She painted the exterior, refinished the floors, and generally tackled a major remodel of her half of the building. She also talked to Judi about the three trees in the backyard and commented they were a little overgrown and wild in her point of view. She convinced Judi to let her "take care of them."

With all the activity going on in her building, Judi went away for a few days. When she came home, she discovered that Trina had removed the trees completely. Judi was horrified.

"I didn't say you could cut down the trees!" she exclaimed to Trina. "I said you could take care of them—that meant *caring* for them. You've ruined the yard. Those were unusual and valuable trees."

"No they weren't!" Trina abruptly replied. "They weren't very special and the yard looks better now, anyway."

"No, it doesn't!" Judi said. "I'm going to check the condominium rules, because I think they say that we must have agreement to do any major work in the common areas of the property."

"Don't be such a jerk about it," Trina said. "You act like you still own the whole place. This half of the duplex is mine, and you're not going to tell me how to live!" And she stormed into her side of the building.

The next thing that Judi noticed was that Trina was playing the piano in her unit late at night. But Trina denied she was playing it at all. Besides, she claimed, the soundproofing she put in would block the sound even if she was playing it. It seemed to Judi that Trina was purposefully being loud to bother her.

At midnight one night, Judi went next door to ask Trina to be quiet. Trina denied making any noise at that time and her boyfriend, who was over, leaned over close to Judi's face and said, "Leave us alone. This house isn't all yours anymore. Stop bossing us around or we'll call the police!"

"Well, please be quiet," Judi said, and left to go back into her unit.

The very next night Judi heard the piano once more until midnight, so she returned to their door to complain. Again, they denied being loud, although they had some music on in the background that seemed pretty loud to Judi. So Judi asked if they could turn down the music.

"No," said Trina's boyfriend. "It's not too loud, we have

soundproofing, and you can't tell us what to do in our own home. If you keep harassing us, I'm going to call the police."

Judi hesitated, because the music still seemed like it was too loud for her to sleep. When she didn't leave immediately, the boyfriend picked up his phone and called the police. When a police officer eventually came, Judi had already returned to her side of the house, but she was still awake.

"What's the trouble?" the officer inquired of Judi. He had already been talking to Trina and her boyfriend.

"My neighbors are playing the piano and other music until midnight and beyond, sometimes. It's really annoying. I can hear it in my side of the duplex."

"Well, they deny they're playing music, and I didn't hear any when I arrived," the officer said.

"Of course, they turned it off, knowing you were coming," Judi said in frustration. "I'm sorry you had to get involved, but I think you'll discover that it's the neighbors who are causing the trouble. I had this duplex made into condos; then she cut down three trees in the backyard without any agreement from me at all. I don't know what to do."

"Well, I can drive by and listen if I get a chance in the later evenings the next few nights that I'm on duty. And you can look up your condo rules and see if she violated them. Maybe you have a small claims case if she did what you said."

"That would be really great!" Judi said. "Of course, they might stay quiet the next few nights. And I'll go back and read the rules. Thanks!"

Judi didn't feel so crazy after talking to the officer. At least he seemed to care, when her neighbor didn't at all. She felt like a prisoner trapped in her own home.

Judi was excited to discover in the condo rules (covenants, conditions, and restrictions, or CC&Rs) that cutting down trees without written permission could require her neighbor to pay her the value of the trees. She looked into her options and tree values, and received an estimate that the trees were worth about $50,000! So she prepared a letter to Trina, requesting that Trina do one of the following options:

- Pay her back for the trees in the amount of $50,000.
- Make a serious proposal regarding the tree removal to Judi that Judi would consider.
- Agree to go to mediation about it.

She offered that Trina could respond by mail, email, or in person.

Then she slipped the letter under Trina's door.

An hour later, there was a loud knocking on Judi's door. It was Trina.

"Are you nuts!" Trina yelled. "There's no f----ing way I'm going to pay you for the work I did in the yard! You have no appreciation at all! You're an a--hole and you'll be sorry if you don't leave me alone. You don't own the whole place anymore. I'll do what I damn well please with *my* home!" And she stormed off before Judi could say anything. Soon Judi could hear loud banging on her piano.

That night there was no music and Judi hoped that was the end of it. But two days later, she received a letter under her door from Trina saying that Judi had violated the CC&Rs and there was supposed to be condo meetings as well as a monthly assessment fee for common property upkeep. Trina demanded that Judi attend a meeting and that Judi make a deposit into the condo fund as the original owner; she also claimed that Judi had violated the rules by not already having a condo fund in place. If Judi was going to bring any legal action, then Trina was as well.

Judi got a lawyer's opinion and decided to have the lawyer write a response to Trina. Perhaps this would calm things down. She didn't want to feel like a prisoner in her own home, but she also didn't think it was right that Trina had cut down the trees with no consequence for it at all. She figured that she would be endlessly harassed if she did not respond but that she would be harassed if she did. She thought about her options and decided to go the legal route—letting a lawyer handle it for her. She decided it was worth the lawyer's fees, which she would ask to be reimbursed along with the tree compensation.

Her lawyer's letter laid out options and added a proposal for arbitration of the tree issue. The next thing Judi knew, she received a letter from a lawyer for Trina, which was much more demanding and threatening. There were little things that Judi had apparently not done or did incorrectly with the condo conversion, for which Trina's lawyer was demanding significant payment to Trina from Judi.

Judi's lawyer said Trina's lawyer was just blowing smoke, but it still worried Judi. They agreed to push for mediation, with arbitration as a backup plan. (Mediation is a method where a mediator (neutral third person) helps the parties make their own decisions. Arbitration has an arbitrator who makes the decisions for the parties.) Judi was looking for some kind of action that would make Trina stop being so awful. She really regretted having done the condo conversion now and was having trouble sleeping at night.

Trina agreed to mediation and she was extremely pleasant in the mediation session, both with the mediator and with Judi. But she calmly held firm that she would not pay a penny as a consequence for removing the trees. She agreed not to play her piano after 10 p.m., unless she was having friends over for a musical evening. This would not happen more than once a month on a weekend, and she would quit playing by midnight at the latest. She would give advance notice to Judi, so she could stay out late on those nights. The two women agreed to these terms during the session.

It was quiet that first night after the mediation session, but the next night Trina played her piano until 10:30, as if to test Judi's tolerance for her breaking their agreement. Judi didn't know what to do, so she called her lawyer and discussed other options. They agreed to pursue arbitration next.

Before the first arbitration session, Trina's lawyer submitted a claim against Judi for nearly $20,000 in damages for violating other matters of the CC&R. Judi's lawyer said those claims were absurd and just a ploy to get leverage in the case. At the initial meeting, the arbitrator said that Judi might have a valid claim for the trees and that they should both submit valuation estimates for them. He said he would need to do some more research on the trees and on Trina's claims. The arbitrator also said that there might be an award of some attorney's fees and requested a detailed listing of what they were. But the arbitrator strongly encouraged them to reach a negotiated settlement before their final full arbitration hearing, after which the arbitrator would make final decisions for them.

That evening, Trina emailed Judi and said, "We should be able to settle this ourselves. It's ridiculous that we're paying attorneys to do this. I'm willing to drop my claims against you if you're willing to drop yours against me."

No way, Judi thought to herself. She smelled victory in the arbitration and saw Trina's email as reinforcing that idea. It was a desperate attempt to sidestep the arbitration, just as her attorney had predicted. But then Judi had another thought.

She wrote back to Trina, "I'm not willing to agree to that, but I would consider other proposals. I've made a lot of proposals to you. Now can you give me a better proposal?"

"I'm thinking of moving," Trina wrote back. "If you drop the case, I'll drop mine and I'll rent to someone else who doesn't play piano."

"Let me think about that," Judi wrote in reply. It didn't take her long to conclude that dealing with Trina as a landlord for tenants next door would likely be an even bigger headache than dealing with her as a neighbor. Trina had repeatedly shown that she would not follow through on her word.

"I can't agree to that," Judi wrote back an hour later. "But I would consider dropping my claims against you if you dropped yours against me and sold your place. You can think about that for a couple days if you want."

The next afternoon Judi received an email from Trina: "I'll sell my place, but I want you to compensate me for my loss, since house values have gone down some since I bought it. And it's because of you that I have to sell it."

Judi wanted to strangle her. But she thought about it—and how long this battle had waged and how long it would potentially take Trina to sell the condo in today's market. After talking to her attorney, she finally wrote back to Trina: "I have a solution. I'll buy it back from you at today's fair market value. My attorney will handle the sale, and that way you won't have any costs of sale. You'll end up with more money than selling it on the open market, and it can be finished in 30 days. Think about it. But let me know by Friday, because I need to prepare for the arbitration."

On Friday, Trina emailed Judi: "My attorney says we could win the arbitration but that for my peace of mind, I should accept your offer. He says you've put me through so much that I should get as far away from you as possible. So he will call your attorney to write up the paperwork, and I will move out over the next 30 days if we can agree on the fair market value you will pay me."

It was fairly easy for the attorneys to agree on a fair market value, which was the same amount that Judi had left in the bank from selling the condo to Trina in the first place. She had spent about 10 percent of it and, although she would end up with nothing to show for all her efforts, she had gotten another job and so would be fine financially. Still, the ordeal ended on a couple of sad notes—she did not have extra money in the bank as she had planned, and she lost the special trees in her backyard, which her parents had planted so many years ago.

The good news was that she would have control over her next-door neighbor—which was worth more than money, she now realized. No more HCPs for her!

Discussion of This Example

This example demonstrates many of the common issues when problem solving and negotiating with an HCP. Trina seems to have many characteristics of a HCP: she easily misinterprets or exaggerates others' statements (permission to "take care of" the trees); she's comfortable yelling and swearing at her neighbor who she hardly knows; she makes little effort to solve problems through communication or compromise; and she seems oblivious to the realistic needs of those around her (loud music). She also has a mean streak, in terms of getting revenge for Judi's feedback by making more noise and violating her own agreements in mediation. Plus, she can be highly manipulative, such as being charming and agreeable while in mediation even though she does necessarily plan to carry out her agreements.

On the other hand, it appears that Judi is not an HCP, as she sought to communicate about problems and was willing to make several proposals throughout the difficulties. She realistically sought advice and assistance (from a lawyer) and never spoke disrespectfully to Trina.

Judi plainly made an effort to give Trina choices by proposing several options to resolve their conflicts. She proposed that Trina simply pay her the full amount of the value of the trees, which is a good negotiating strategy with anyone—start out by asking for what you fully want; then be open to some give-and-take to resolve the issue at a lesser amount or on terms that you are acceptable to you. What Judi did was invite Trina to make a "serious proposal" back to her if she didn't agree.

Some traditional negotiators might say that Judi should not have given her that option right after making her own proposal— that she should have simply waited for Trina to respond, so she didn't appear to give in too easily. However, when you are dealing with an HCP, it is often more important to emphasize that you are willing to work with the person rather than taking a rigid position.

You can still be firm and say, "No, I can't go that far. I do have my limits. But I am willing to listen to offers within a realistic range."

Judi also wasn't willing to do all of the negotiation work. She said to Trina when they were emailing: "I've made a lot of proposals to you. Now can you give me a better proposal?" This shows that it doesn't hurt to start out being the one to make proposals in some situations, but that you shouldn't do all the work yourself—you can ask the other person to make a proposal. This is especially important when dealing with an HCP, as they often prefer that you do all the work on solving the problem. Yet they aren't committed to the solution unless they played a part in creating it.

Lastly, this example shows how Judi took action to set limits on Trina's aggressive behavior—by reading the rules (the CC&Rs), talking with a lawyer, and ultimately submitting a legal claim to an arbitrator. While her action got a flurry of negative responses from Trina and her lawyer, it ultimately became clear that Judi might win the case. HCPs often don't pull back their aggressive behavior until they are facing real negative consequences. So long as it's about arguing and controlling conversations, HCPs can be very comfortable. But when real positive or negative consequences stare them down, they often become much more realistic. Only when she faced serious consequences for her actions did Trina begin making and considering realistic proposals.

Summary

This chapter has demonstrated how a reasonable person can use proposals to manage a conflict with an HCP and to move toward resolution rather than getting stuck in arguments or just giving up. Asking the other person, especially an HCP, to make proposals engages that person in the solution. That's why it's important that the reasonable person avoid doing all the work.

This chapter has also showed why it's important to set limits and communicate those limits seriously to an HCP—and safely through a third party, if necessary, such as having a lawyer do the communicating. This can make proposals become more realistic to and from an HCP.

It helps, of course, for the lawyer to be skilled at dealing with HCPs as well, rather than unnecessarily increasing the conflict, as Trina's lawyer seemed to do. It also helps when decision makers, such as an arbitrator or judge, give the parties a reality check but then encourage them to continue negotiating—since HCPs are more likely to accept a decision they participate in making rather than one imposed by someone else.

Unfortunately, this chapter has also showed how extreme and dangerous HCPs can be as neighbors. There can be constant conflicts over noise, parking, trees, home appearance, and all styles of living in close quarters. It's especially important not to angrily confront an HCP, but to instead get assistance and develop strategies for calming conflicts and solving problems. Finding a balance of proposing realistic options (which may include setting practical limits) and respectfully seeking the HCP's realistic options can help.

CHAPTER NINE

Volunteer and Nonprofit Organizations

V olunteer work can be one of the most meaningful parts
of our lives. Anyone can volunteer, regardless of how rich
or poor they are, how skilled or unskilled, or how much
or little time they have available. This is the good news. The bad
news is that volunteer organizations attract many HCPs, precisely
because these organizations routinely accept anyone committed to
the group's "cause." Volunteer roles are less defined than in a paid
job, and people come and go so quickly that few people may realize
that there is an HCP in the group—until they're unpleasantly
surprised. People are caught off guard by their extreme behavior
and many may just quit the organization or move to a different task
away from the HCP, rather than deal with the high-conflict person.

Nonprofit organizations, including hospitals, universities,
churches, synagogues, mosques, and other non-governmental
agencies, face a similar problem. They have a "larger purpose" and
usually tolerate HCP behavior far too long in an effort to be "nice"
and non-confrontational toward someone who is "one of us." It's
not unusual for HCPs to stay in their positions or to move up in
these organizations because no one confronts them openly. They
sometimes become embedded in positions of authority and this
makes it very difficult to remove them.

Top administrators in nonprofit organizations are often
overwhelmed with funding and other issues, so they don't want to
rock the boat by firing or disciplining key personnel. But frequently,
top administrators don't even know how troublesome some of their
middle managers may be, because they are so good at "talking the
talk" of the organization's public purpose. Employees below them
often are afraid to speak out or it's just not in their nature to make

a fuss, as they are the "good people" of the organization. So these HCPs often carry on by "kicking down" and "kissing up."

The "Helpful" Volunteer

Fred joined the newsletter committee of his statewide volunteer organization. At his first meeting, he had lots of ideas and couldn't keep from interrupting everyone else.

"You have to totally revise the newsletter," Fred said. "It looks terrible—like it's still in the dark ages! You have to do it this way. . . And that way. . ." He went on and on.

Whenever someone else mentioned an idea, he would interrupt and start giving his opinion of how it should be done. The meeting ended earlier than usual, with very little getting accomplished.

Ray, the newsletter editor, was totally frustrated. He confided in one of the other committee members: "I'm thinking of just quitting the committee. I don't know how to deal with Fred. I've never met someone so disruptive at a meeting, and yet he seems like a smart guy. One of his ideas was actually quite good. If I stay on, I wonder if we need to kick him off the committee."

The other member replied: "He does have some good ideas, even if he can't control himself. Maybe there's a way to manage him, so that we can get the benefit of his good ideas without his disruptive behavior."

Ray investigated ways to deal with difficult people and arranged for a consultation with someone who coaches people in managing "high-conflict" personalities.

Coach: "It's important that you don't just try to stop Fred. Instead, suggest a better behavior to do. For example, you could say, 'Fred, your concerns are important. It would be easier to absorb them if you could write them down and send them to all of us before the next meeting. Then we could really think about them.' He may or may not write anything, but it puts the burden on him to solve this in a more productive way—without simply

SO, WHAT'S YOUR PROPOSAL?

challenging him and increasing his defensiveness."

Ray: "But what if he keeps interrupting and trying to change the subject?"

Coach: "Just gently tell him that's not the topic on your agenda right now. He'll have to save it for later. That way, you're not just shutting him down—which he'll get more defensive about—but are redirecting him to a different time to raise his concerns. High-conflict people do better when you redirect them, rather than just trying to get them to stop; that only increases their anxiety and desperation to talk more. Give it a try."

Ray: "I'm not sure I can be so 'gentle' about it, but I'll try your theory."

At the next meeting, Ray said, "We've got a lot to cover, so I'm going to stick closely to our agenda. Let's try to stay focused. Everyone okay with that?" Everyone nodded yes.

In the middle of the first topic, Fred interrupted, "You're really thinking too small here everybody. The problem isn't just the financial page—it's the whole format of the newsletter. We're not going to get any respect without a complete overhaul and—"

This time, Ray quickly interrupted, "Fred, that's not on the agenda. Right now we're just talking about the financial page. If you have something to say about that, go ahead. Otherwise, you need to wait."

Fred, getting louder, said, "But you can't talk about one page before talking about the format of the whole newsletter!"

Ray replied, "Yes, we can—"

"But you're missing the point!" Fred insisted.

Ray calmly explained, "Fred, that is not on the agenda for right now. If you want to add something after we go through the whole agenda, we'll see if we have time. Or maybe next time."

Fred, turning to the others in the group, asked, "What do you think? Don't you think that we should be discussing the whole format first?"

"Fred, stop!" Ray said. "I am the editor and I'm running this meeting! You have some good ideas, but you're off the topic for now, so you'll need to wait."

"But—" Fred said, still trying to take over the discussion.

Ray cut him off: "Fred, just stop! Make some notes and save it for later. Thank you. Now who wants to go next with comments about the financial page?"

Fortunately, someone jumped in with ideas about this topic. Fred squirmed in his seat, but he stayed quiet. Everyone wondered if he would walk out. Ray proceeded to control the meeting and the room slowly relaxed. Fred even made some "on topic" contributions later in the meeting.

After the meeting, Ray spoke with one of the other members. "What do you think of how the meeting went?" he asked.

The committee member, Samuel, replied, "I think you did great! I wanted to strangle Fred, but you actually calmed him down and he became more productive. I thought you would have to kick him out, but you actually managed to get him to behave. What do you think?"

"I'm really surprised that he accepted my direction and I'm surprised he didn't walk out," Ray said. "I just tried to focus on what I wanted him to do, rather than what he was doing wrong. I kept trying to give him something *to do*, rather than just telling him to shut up."

"And it seemed to work," Samuel said.

Ray said, "Yes. For now. We'll see how it goes next time."

Surprisingly, next time Fred focused on the topic and never challenged Ray again. He participated inconsistently on the newsletter committee, but his contributions were taken seriously—some of which the group found useful. It was as if he just needed people to know he was important enough to be listened to. And Ray consistently sent out a clear agenda to the committee before each meeting—and he made sure to stick to it.

Discussion of This Example

This example demonstrates how redirecting a potential HCP to another choice or task, rather than just trying to stop him, can yield effective results. This is very important with HCPs, because they often lack the impulse control to stop themselves—and they easily get highly defensive if you challenge them aggressively (even if they are challenging you aggressively). So diverting them into a more productive task is much simpler and may help bring out their best behavior, while avoiding their worst.

Of course, this "redirecting" approach isn't guaranteed to be successful and some HCPs may have to be kicked out of a volunteer organization completely. Otherwise, they may be so disruptive that all the volunteers leave. But this example shows that some potential HCPs can do well with a strong structure, which Ray learned to provide. Ironically, HCPs point you toward the structure you need to use with them. In this case, the editor needed to restrain Fred from talking "off topic" because he couldn't restrain himself.

While Ray redirected Fred without offering him a choice, the choice was implied. ("If you don't do this other behavior, I will have to evict you from the meeting.") With HCPs, it is often best to avoid talking about the negative choice; otherwise it may make the HCP think about it more and lead them to do it—as though it were a challenge! It's better just to focus on the desired behavior without saying much more. HCPs are very sensitive to negative judgments and negative tones of voice. Here is how Ray expressed the desired behaviors in this case:

- "If you want to add something after we go through the whole agenda, we'll see if we have time. Or maybe next time."

And,

- "Make some notes and save it for later."

Negative Advocates

Another issue arose in this case: Fred turned to the rest of the group to try to get their support against what Ray was saying. In high-conflict cases, this is often seen as trying to recruit "negative advocates." Negative advocates are people who totally agree with and support HCPs, and make excuses for them or try to protect them from the negative consequences of their actions. Negative advocates are often emotionally hooked by the HCP's intense charm or intense fear or anger against someone else. This intensity can be so persuasive that some people become negative advocates for HCPs and become highly vocal in arguing their cases for them, including in the workplace, in communities, and in families. This can include professionals, such as lawyers and counselors, who are not aware of this dynamic and get swept up into fighting for the wrong "victim" or "cause," since they are uninformed about the full and true situation. Negative advocates can be very persuasive to others, when the HCP on his or her own lacks credibility. But if negative advocates become informed, they often disappear or turn on the HCP in anger at being misled.

Anyone can become a negative advocate. However, some of these advocates have their own high-conflict personalities—in this way, HCPs often find each other. Indeed, high-conflict people can be strongly attracted to each other and become a team, which makes life even more difficult for those around them, such as in an organization or large family. Of course, people with high-conflict personalities can also split up with the same intensity that they found each other.

Fortunately for Ray the editor, Fred did not hook anyone into becoming his negative advocate. But just imagine how much more difficult it would have become if Fred got another volunteer to say, "Yeah, Ray! Fred's right! We should scrap this agenda and talk about what Fred wants to discuss!"

In general, the best way to deal with negative advocates is the same way as dealing with an HCP: Treat them with empathy and respect, and focus them on information and the choices that they can make.

The Board

Peaceful Meadows is a nonprofit retirement community operated by a large church. The board of directors is responsible for its overall management, and the CEO is responsible for the daily operations and is accountable to the board. They have quarterly meetings in person, and much board business is handled by committees in between these meetings.

Joseph Miller is the CEO. Recently he received a formal letter from a new resident in the community, Lawrence Carter. Carter had been the dean of the local law school, and he was not happy to be moving into the retirement community after his wife of 47 years passed away six months ago and he sold his home to move into Peaceful Meadows. He was only 79 years old. His letter said the following:

Dear Mr. Miller:

I moved into Peaceful Meadows exactly 30 days ago. I have observed numerous problems with your organization and I demand that they be addressed and resolved if I am going to continue to reside here. If they are not resolved appropriately, I will report these problems to the powers that be and I can assure you that heads will roll.

Problem 1: The grounds! It's hard for me to believe how shabby this place is. The flower beds include drooping flowers, the grass grows too high before it gets mowed, and the trees need trimming. It's a disgrace to be associated with such carelessness. I'm starting to think of this place as Careless Meadows.

Problem 2: The noise! Yesterday was the last straw! There were workmen in the hallway pounding right near my room for hours in the afternoon. I need to take a nap each afternoon and this ruined my sleep, which ruined my day.

Problem 3: Electric carts! Everyone knows there are at least three residents who drive electric carts in the hallways. They are a terrible hazard. I use a cane and I walk slower than I used to. Two days ago I was horrified to witness a resident backing out of the elevator right into another resident (her husband, no less—also with a cane), knocking him down and almost sending him tumbling down the stairway across from the elevator. I am sure you would not like to have this reported to the larger church community.

Problem 4: Pets! I understand that Careless Meadows allows small dogs, cats, and birds as pets. I was sitting outside on a bench in the gardens last week and this horrid little dog came up to me and tried to lick my hand. I can't imagine the unsanitary possibilities in this community if pets can go around licking one person's hand after another. Who knows what diseases could get spread quickly through an entire community.

Problem 5: Being ignored! I moved in 30 days ago and I still have not had a personal visit from the CEO—you! When a man of my stature moves in, I would have expected some personal recognition. One day you walked right by the lunchroom when I was there and you didn't come over to talk to me. I felt very disrespected.

You must do something about these problems or I will leave and inform the larger church community of why I did!

Sincerely,

Dean Lawrence Carter

cc: Mr. Harold Harbour, President of the Board of Directors
     Mrs. Rhonda Rice, Secretary of the Board

Whew! Joseph thought. *What a jerk! Give me a break! I finally had a vacation, and now when I return he says that I'm the problem—I should have been here the whole time holding his hand! Oops, but those thoughts aren't very kind. He's probably upset about all these changes. But I do need to manage this or it could blow up. I better to talk to Harold before the next board meeting next week. I'm certain that Rhonda will copy this to all of the board members.*

The next board meeting was a little rocky.

"I know Dean Carter," said one member. "And it bothers me to hear that we are failing him. He has come to us in his time of need, and Joseph shouldn't have ignored him and let these problems grow."

"Wait a minute," said another member. "Joseph is doing a wonderful job, and Dean Carter is being extremely rude to all of us to threaten us this way."

"You don't sound very caring," snapped the first member.

"And you don't sound very respectful of Joseph," the other snapped back. "It's not that hard to find new residents, but it is hard to find a CEO as skilled as Joseph. If we're taking sides, I'm on Joseph's side on this one. And I think the grounds look lovely! The nerve of that man—"

"Hold on, folks!" Harold, the board president interrupted. "We're starting to get into 'splitting' here and that's not good."

"What's splitting?" another member asked.

Team Splitting

"Splitting is when a professional team splits in half and each side starts hating the other half," Harold said. "It happens when there's someone in the community with a high-conflict personality. It's a concept that was first discovered in hospital treatment programs when someone with a personality disorder was a patient. I learned about that when I was on the board of one of our hospitals and one of our substance abuse units had this problem.

"It was originally called 'staff splitting,' because the staff would split over what the proper care of the patient should be. Half the staff starts thinking we have to go real easy on the patient and be very supportive. The other half of the staff feels that we have to really challenge the patient to make big changes or consider kicking them out of the unit.

"It's not at all surprising that our discussion this morning already split into those members who are very supportive of Dean Carter and those who are being very supportive of Joseph. The solution is to define the problem as not an 'either/or' problem—good guy versus bad guy—but rather as figuring out how to deal with both aspects: how to be supportive of Dean Carter while also being supportive of Joseph and the good work he's done for us here.

"So I propose that Joseph quickly talk directly with Dean Carter and ease their relationship. A little attention will probably go a long way, especially if he might have a high-conflict personality. But we need to keep in mind that he may not be a high-conflict person at all and instead is just feeling very vulnerable right now because of losing his wife and having to lose his home and routines by moving in here with us. But whether he's a high-conflict person or not, Joseph can use his excellent people skills to really connect with the dean and also look into the problems he has. And I would suggest, Joseph, that you ask the dean to give you some suggestions for how *he* would solve these problems. If we can engage him in the solutions, then he is less likely to stay focused on the problems."

The board unanimously passed a motion that Joseph speak immediately and directly with Carter to address ways of resolving the problems he raised.

"Dean Carter," Joseph said, when the dean opened the door to his large room, which was crammed with belongings from the home he had just sold. "I'm so pleased to meet you. Can we talk for a bit? Am I interrupting anything?"

"No, not at all. Do come in!" he was very welcoming and did

not appear to be angry with Joseph.

"I was so sorry to hear about your wife. How long were you together?"

"Almost 50 years," Carter said, with tears welling up in his eyes. "It's really hard without her. And it's really hard fitting into this small space. I've had to give up so much."

"I know what that's like," Joseph said sympathetically.

"No, you don't!" Carter cut him short, angrily. "You don't know what it's like. How could you?"

"You're right . . . I don't know exactly what that's like. It must be awful in ways I can't imagine. I guess we're never prepared for a time like this."

"You've got that right," Carter softened. "Now I suppose you're here because of my letter."

"Yes, but I also did want to take some time to meet you and get to know you, now that I'm back from my vacation. I was so busy before I left. But I do feel bad that we didn't get off on a good start and I'm ready to do that now. I appreciated your letter and I am looking into the problems you raised. We really value resident feedback."

"We'll see," said Carter, sternly. "You do agree with me that these are big problems, don't you?"

"I'm looking into all of them now. And I wanted to suggest that we value your input so much that I would encourage you to write us a letter with a list of *your* suggestions for solving each of these problems. It's not unusual that our residents come up with really good ideas, based on their own direct experience. Would you consider doing that?"

"Yes, of course!" Carter smiled. "Funny, but that's what I used to say to my professors at the law school when they would tell me about a problem. I would say, 'If you're going to tell me about a problem, you have to tell me about a proposed solution— or I won't listen to the problem!' There was one professor who hated that, said it was my job to come up with solutions. Hah! I mostly ignored him. He was a difficult person. Do you think I'm a difficult person?"

This caught Joseph off guard. "I don't think so! If we're having this kind of conversation, then I don't think that either one of us could be a difficult person. After all, we're talking about solutions, aren't we?"

"Yes, we are."

"So, I really am interested in your suggestions to the problems you raised—and any future problems. We're not perfect here, but we really do try hard. I hope you'll give us a chance."

Two days later, Joseph received another letter from Dean Lawrence Carter:

Dear Mr. Miller:

I was pleased to meet you on Tuesday. I enjoyed our discussion and look forward to having more.

You asked me to give you some suggestions for the problems I brought to your attention. Here they are as "proposed solutions" after each problem.

Problem 1: The grounds! It's hard for me to believe how shabby this place is. The flower beds include drooping flowers, the grass grows too high before it gets mowed, and the trees need trimming. It's a disgrace to be associated with such carelessness. I'm starting to think of this place as Careless Meadows.

Proposed solution 1: I suggest that the grass be mowed at least every two weeks. You water a lot and the grass grows quickly. The flower beds should be attended to every day, so that the drooping flowers can be removed right away. And just get those trees trimmed. That should last a long time, but they've been ignored for quite a while, I'll bet.

Problem 2: The noise! Yesterday was the last straw! There were workmen in the hallway pounding right near my room for hours in the afternoon. I need to take a nap each afternoon and this ruined my sleep, which ruined my day.

Proposed solution 2: Don't have workmen do any pounding in the afternoon in the hallways. Many of us take naps then! In the morning or during meals is the best time, because I am out of my room during those times.

Problem 3: Electric carts! Everyone knows there are at least three residents who drive electric carts in the hallways. They are a terrible hazard. I use a cane and I walk slower than I used to. Two days ago I was horrified to witness a resident backing out of the elevator right into another resident (her husband, no less—also with a cane), knocking him down and almost sending him tumbling down the stairway across from the elevator. I am sure you would not like to have this reported to the larger church community.

Proposed solution 3: You should give a regular driver's test to those using electric carts. You should also require them to back into the elevators, so that when they come out they can easily see what is in front of them.

Problem 4: Pets! I understand that Careless Meadows allows small dogs, cats, and birds as pets. I was sitting outside on a bench in the gardens last week and this horrid little dog came up to me and tried to lick my hand. I can't imagine the unsanitary possibilities in this community if pets can go around licking one person's hand after another. Who knows what diseases could get spread quickly through an entire community.

Proposed solution 4: Require residents to keep their dogs on leashes and close to their owners, so that they aren't licking the hands of other residents who don't particularly like having their hands licked.

Problem 5: Being ignored! I moved in 30 days ago and I still have not had a personal visit from the CEO—you! When a man of my stature moves in, I would have expected some personal recognition. One day you walked right by the lunchroom when I was there and you didn't come over to talk to me. I felt very disrespected.

Proposed solution 5: I think this has been resolved—at least for now. I'm glad that Mr. Miller had a nice vacation.

Sincerely,
Dean Lawrence Carter
cc: Mr. Harold Harbour, President of the Board of Directors
    Mrs. Rhonda Rice, Secretary of the Board

Joseph particularly noticed that Carter had removed his sentence about threatening to move out of the community. He felt much more hopeful about his relationship with the dean and less fearful that he would be generating public controversy about Peaceful Meadows. And he actually found that he liked the guy! Maybe he wasn't going to be a difficult person. But just to be safe, he would say "Hi" on a regular basis. In fact, Joseph decided that he would say "Hi" to all the residents on a more regular basis. He figured that he would rather take the extra time to hear their complaints than have them come in writing and copied to the board.

Discussion of This Example

In terms of asking for proposals, this was a classic case of turning complaints and blame into proposals. Like the complaints in this case, many complaints made to organizations today arrive in formal written letters, as well as in emails and voicemail messages. In many situations, they call for a written response that is Brief, Informative, Friendly, and Firm. (For more on these BIFF Responses, see the book *BIFF: Quick Responses to High-Conflict People.*)

However, in this case, Joseph really needed to respond to the complaints in person and this went quite well. Since being personally ignored was Dean Carter's biggest issue, giving him personal attention was a very important response. It was interesting that Carter did not respond angrily to Joseph and instead responded quite well to his attention. This is very common with HCPs, who seem extremely angry in writing but can be very friendly and positive in person. It's as though writing is a safer method for them to express anger, which is why emails can be so hostile even coming from people who are generally nice in person.

Joseph could have started out by being very defensive and justifying his lack of contact with the dean. After all, he was very busy before his vacation and then he was gone. The timing of Carter's arrival was unfortunate, but things like this happen—they can't all be prevented. The solution is to quickly respond in a positive manner when such a complaint is made, and then to shift the discussion away from the past and onto proposals for the future.

The subject of "team splitting" arose in this case. It is surprisingly common in volunteer groups, nonprofit organizations, religious organizations, universities, and health care settings. The reason for this seems to be that they are open to anyone and place a high value on accepting who people are, rather than criticizing or expelling them. Then, when a high-conflict person starts getting attention, those working with the HCP absorb the "split" that the HCP already has set in his or her own mind; namely, that some people are "all-good" and some people are "all-bad." They act toward those in the team around them in this manner, treating some in a very friendly "you're-the-best" way and others in a very negative "you're-the-worst" way.

Team members then emotionally absorb this split and start seeing each other as "all-good" and "all-bad," usually based on the "supportive approach" versus the "challenging approach" to the HCP as the sides of the split. When professionals and others don't realize this is happening, they can get very angry and resentful toward each other. If they know about this dynamic, however, the split usually evaporates very quickly—as the team discusses an approach to treating the person with a balance of realistic support and realistic challenges.

Lastly, the question of whether Dean Carter is really a high-conflict person arises in this case. HCPs have a pattern of frequently blaming others and using a lot of all-or-nothing thinking, unmanaged emotions, and extreme behaviors. However, we don't yet know whether this behavior by Carter was simply because of the *situation* he was in—losing his wife and moving out of his large home into a one-room unit in a retirement community. Only time will tell. But in terms of using this method of asking "So, what's your proposal?" it doesn't matter. It can be used with any upset person, whether or not they have a high-conflict pattern.

Summary

This chapter has pointed out how HCPs often show up in volunteer groups and nonprofit organizations: as clients, as team members, and sometimes as leaders. Realizing this likelihood and teaching everyone involved about these dynamics can make the difference between a well-functioning and satisfying group effort or chaos, resentment, and even the demise of an organization.

The practice of asking "So, what's your proposal?" can be used to manage a disruptive member during group meetings or as a way to draw out good ideas that an organization can use from potentially high-conflict members. The goal is to limit the high-conflict behavior while getting the most out of members and staff.

Of course, there will be some HCPs who will need to leave the organization if the organization is to survive. But I believe that in the majority of HCP cases, it is possible to manage HCPs so that they don't disrupt the group and can contribute positively to the work that everyone wants to accomplish. Managing them well just takes practice. This is especially important in organizations where conflicts can arise easily and quickly. By simply and calmly asking for proposed solutions, the controversy can often be calmed and many problems may be solved.

CHAPTER TEN

Participating in Politics

Politics and government are both a location of many high-conflict people and a "target of blame" for many HCPs outside of the government and major political processes. Recent years have seen several governors and mayors being pressured to step down for probable HCP behavior—including lying, cheating, overexposing themselves on the Internet, harassing women, smoking crack, and other extreme behaviors. Many of them have a pattern of high-conflict behavior that is shocking to the public, but not to dispute resolution professionals who have been dealing with high-conflict personalities for years.

Can these extreme HCPs be effectively managed by asking them "So, what do you propose?" It's hard to say, because so many factors impact today's politicians: exposure in the news media, the 24/7 news cycle, international events (such as 9/11), frequent elections, constant fund-raising for elections, and so forth. Politicians certainly engage in "splitting," which was described in the previous chapter: they blow their own horns as the "all-good" politicians and rip apart others as the "all-bad" politicians. The effect of this has been to reduce the number of moderates in state legislatures and Congress in Washington, DC.

In terms of getting work done in Congress in the 2012–2014 term, the House of Representatives has produced "the lowest number of legislative *proposals* since the Clinton administration" in the 1990s, as reported by the New York Times (emphasis added). It's fascinating—and not surprising—to see that with the increase of likely HCPs in Congress, we have a decrease in "legislative proposals." There are fewer politicians asking "So, what's your proposal?" and more politicians taking all-or-nothing positions.

Why is this happening? As Ross Baker, a congressional expert at Rutgers University in New Brunswick, N.J. recently explained, "So little of what Congress does is legislation and so much of what it does is message." The behavior and strategy all seem geared to winning the next election, rather than doing anything while they are in Congress. This fits with HCP thinking: "We're all-good, and they're all-bad. So vote for me." That's the message.

Of course, the reality is that they can't possibly succeed at winning big with this behavior, because no party permanently wins a seat and each party can undermine the other's efforts, because of how voting districts are mapped out and how the rules operate in Congress. Either party can disrupt the other, although it takes two to accomplish very much—which is why so little is getting accomplished in this decade. With the heavy influence of the media, it appears that being a star is more important than getting work done. Thus, narcissistic HCPs appear to be entering politics in record numbers, while reasonable people are avoiding this whole "game."

Let the Public Participate

I believe that one of the reasons for high-conflict political behavior is that the public actually wants to be more involved in making decisions for themselves and their cities/states/countries than ever before. Participation may be the most important word in politics today, and we see this regularly in world events. With the rise of instant mass communication and scientific knowledge, it is possible for a large number of people to become informed and speak out on many key issues. (We no longer have representatives riding horses to Philadelphia to write the Constitution and returning to their states several months later.)

However, with much of the population having little direct experience with making political proposals or decisions, they are easily swayed by the simplicity and intensity of many politicians with HCP characteristics. The public may be swayed by all-or-nothing arguments, especially when they are repeated and repeated in the 24/7 media.

Yet this drive to participate will continue to grow stronger and hopefully will bring more political education and problem-solving skills for the general public. With that in mind, politicians should consider ways to educate the public and involve their constituents more, rather than less, in decision making. This may also be a way of reducing political polarization, because today's general population is considered to be more moderate than today's politicians.

The City Council

The debate over the minimum wage provides a classic example of how participation by the largest group possible is impacting an issue. Imagine the following:

"The current minimum wage for our state is $8 per hour," said the city councilman. "This is absurd in an economy where the richest 1 percent has made huge profits and dramatic increases in their total wealth while the average and lower income worker is barely making it at all. The least we could do for the people who elected us is to raise the minimum wage to $13 over the next three years. This is the amount a recent study said our citizens would need to simply make ends meet."

"Such a move would destroy our economy," said a city councilwoman. "I'm absolutely opposed to any effort to raise the minimum wage. It would inspire employers to stop covering health insurance, home health care would become unaffordable for many who need it, small businesses might leave the city or be undermined, companies would have to raise prices—basically, a disaster. It shouldn't be raised at all."

"But we have the votes," the city councilman said. "We're the city's representatives. We should do what we were elected to do—make decisions!"

The city attorney spoke up: "The councilman is correct. The city council does have the authority to raise the minimum wage on its own. However, there's a state proposition going on the ballot that would raise it to $10 an hour over the next three years. In general, you're better off having a public discussion and public vote on something like this. It makes the decision more stable and less vulnerable to being set aside or overruled by the next city council, when there isn't a majority in favor of a higher minimum wage. They might simply reverse your victory—possibly leaving the people worse off. With a statewide proposition, it would take a new ballot initiative to overturn the decision in the future if the political tides turned, and that is much more difficult. I would recommend that you defer this to the state vote as a compromise. The proposed ballot proposition will have exceptions for some businesses that would be the most vulnerable to leaving the city and struggling to meet a higher payroll."

"But we were elected as a majority to do what is in the best interests of the city," the councilman exclaimed loudly. "Our voters will be much better off with a $13 minimum wage!"

"Let's take a recess," the city attorney suggested. He caught the eye of the councilman and indicated he'd like to talk with him privately.

"We were elected to do a job and a lot of my voters need some financial help!" the councilman explained when meeting alone with the city attorney. "I don't care if we have to shove it down the other side's throats. We have the votes and I want to do it now, while we can. You're trying to tie my hands."

"No," said the attorney. "I'm really thinking ahead of the consequences that may actually help you. If you shove it down the others' throats, they will spend the next election cycle telling all the voters that the city government is taking away their ability to vote on this and shoving it down *their throats* and that government can't be trusted.

"You know how popular that idea is right now nationwide. That would weaken everything we're both trying to do, even though we're from different parties—though everyone knows

I'm a moderate (one of the few left, I think!). I think it's in your political interest, as well as the city's interest as a whole, to have this issue resolved by the general population. That way, you don't get blamed for the outcome—the state voters decided—and it results in more political stability. This is such a volatile, hot-button issue that voters could hang you for it someday. Save council votes mostly for the business that people don't much care about. If you feel strongly on an issue, educate them rather than just deciding it for them and creating your own backlash.

"Remember, I'm the one telling you that you have the authority to do this, but I'm recommending that on this issue you should show restraint and go with the state ballot proposition. The voters overall will thank you for respecting them enough to make this decision themselves. You come out looking wise and restrained, since you have the power to shove it down our throats but didn't do it. Think long-term. You have a long potential political career ahead of you. That's my advice."

"Hmm," the councilman said with a sigh. "I guess I'll think about it and discuss it with the others. I can agree to table it for today."

"It's up to you," the attorney smiled. "It's just a recommendation from me."

Discussion of This Example

First, are the two city council members high-conflict people? Or are they simply passionate about their issues and representing their voters? Remember: It doesn't matter. What's important is handling situations like this with methods that help resolve conflict thoughtfully rather than by simply reacting.

In this case, the city attorney discussed the two main choices that the councilman was facing and hoped to explain why the consequence of one was much better than the other. He was trying to get him thinking. One of the key points that he made was how sensitive today's electorate is about the role of government and elected officials.

By applying the same HCP principles that we have been discussing, the attorney may have helped his colleague avoid the trap of making decisions *for* others and then getting blamed for those decisions. By saving the decision for the voters, and explaining why (because it was so important as a public policy issue), the councilman would be able to look honorable in the eyes of the electorate. Otherwise, he might seem to be a bully trying to get his way and keeping others out of the process.

Whatever you think about this issue or other major policy issues, the political dilemma of our age seems to be whether to fight for victories that may later be undone or to engage the larger group or population in a slower but more stable process of decision making. Given the recent trends in Congress and the public's low opinion of it, this seems like a good time to try an approach that we have learned from dealing with HCPs—the more they participate in finding the solution, the more they tend to accept the outcome.

The "Third Rail" of Politics

There may not be a hot-button issue in American politics that's more divisive than Social Security—the federally funded retirement-age income program that was started in the 1930s. It will reportedly run out of money in 2033, because there are more people retiring in relation to the number of workers paying into the program—plus, retirees are living longer. For decades, politicians on the right have argued that it should be eliminated in favor of individualized retirement savings while politicians on the left have argued that it should be left alone as is. The general public is very protective of the program, but also worried about its unstable future.

Some politicians have lost elections because of their apparent position on this single issue. Indeed, taking a vocal stance on Social Security can be political death. That's why it's called a "third rail" issue, using a railroad metaphor for the rail that provides electricity for electric trains, with enough power to kill someone if they touch it. But suppose that the voters got together and pressured their representatives to actually negotiate and resolve the future of Social Security. "So, what's your proposal?" the public could ask politicians who take all-or-nothing positions on the subject. If the politicians got serious, the discussion might go like this:

Democrat: "I think we could save money by reducing the benefits of the top 25 percent of earners. They have enough money, so Social Security doesn't mean much to them. With this reduction, we could avoid cutting benefits to the lower 75 percent, many of whom really do rely on it as retirement-age income. That's my proposal."

Republican: "Well, I don't think that picking on the well-to-do is a good policy, as they create so much of the nation's overall income. You don't want to punish them for their success. I would propose that we raise the retirement age to 68, from the current 66 for older boomers and 67 for younger boomers and those younger. That's how you could save some serious money and people who are 66 and 67 are still generally healthy and can still work."

Democrat: "Well, I don't like that. I think that it would be a lot more beneficial to raise the cap on the income subject to the payroll tax to $215,000—so people with income up to that amount would keep having Social Security deducted from their paychecks. This is a much higher cap than the present ceiling and those in the higher income brackets could easily afford this."

Republican: "Again, you're punishing the people who create wealth in this country. I think it would be better to raise the rate of payroll tax for Social Security for everyone from 6.2 percent to 6.6 percent. It's a small adjustment that could be shared by everyone."

Republican: "Let's ask a financial analyst which of these proposals would save the most money."

Analyst: "I'm afraid you would have to do all four of these proposals to have a serious impact on the problem. By combining all four of your proposals, the nation would save over 70 percent of the shortfall, but not all of it. You would need to do even more."

Democrat: "Then I would say that we should lift the cap entirely on income subject to the Social Security payroll tax, instead of not taxing those with over $215,000 income per year. Why should wealthier people avoid paying in 6.6 percent of their income to the system that has brought such stability to the country? That would be in everyone's interest."

Republican: "I don't like it, but what impact would that have on the shortfall?" He turned toward the analyst.

Analyst: "That would do it. All of these proposals put together would eliminate the problem."

Democrat: "While I don't like parts of this, if we could sell this to the public as a package, maybe they would tolerate it. We've got to do something sooner rather than later."

Republican: "Yes, but I don't think I could sell this package to my constituents—let alone my colleagues. I'd never live it down and I don't think that you could either."

Democrat: "You're probably right. The public is so angry these days, we may be better off just blaming each other for everything and sticking to our totally opposite positions. But let's quietly do some polling and see what the public really thinks."

The reality is that this invented dialogue is based on a real study sponsored by Voice of the People, a group "which seeks to give informed public opinion a greater voice," and Program for Public Consultation, affiliated with the University of Maryland. They brought together 738 people who represented the American public, educated them about the problems of Social Security, and asked them to "seriously think through the options for dealing with the shortfall."

The result was that 75 percent or more of *both* Democrats and Republicans agreed on all of the first four proposals above:

• Reduce Social Security benefits for the top 25 percent of earners.

• Raise the retirement age to 68 for full benefits.

- Raise the cap on income subject to Social Security payroll tax to $215,000.
- Rate the payroll tax rate for Social Security to 6.6 percent from the current 6.2 percent.

A slight majority of those from *both parties* also agreed to remove the cap on income subject to the payroll tax altogether, which combined with the other proposals would totally eliminate the shortfall.

This study found that average Americans don't just think of themselves—they also consider the common good. Those with higher incomes "were just as likely to favor raising the cap on taxable income" and those under age 48 "were just as likely to favor raising the retirement age." They concluded, "Rather than holding Congress back from making difficult decisions, an informed public may actually help lead the way."

Discussion of This Example

This real-life example shows that reasonable people making proposals and analyzing them can come to agreement by sacrificing some of their self-interest for the "common good." This may come as a surprise to those who watch the continual stream of news about polarization in Congress. Politicians may be becoming more narcissistic and "high-conflict," taking extreme positions and making lots of noise about them. But the people in general— if they are fully educated about an issue and trained in making proposals—may be able to help make good decisions.

Wider participation by the public in politics may be the way that HCP politicians can be reined in, rather than having them dominate Congress and today's public discussions—something which is reinforced, rather than discouraged, by the news media. It will be a great day when news reporters at press conferences shout out, "So, what's your proposal?" whenever HCP politicians get up and blame each other.

Final Proposal

We live in a culture of blame and disrespect. High-conflict people seem to be increasing. Yet we can individually turn around many blaming conversations by simply and respectfully asking "So, what do you propose?"

Of course, this takes practice, which is what this book has been about. After reading through numerous examples, I hope that you have become comfortable with the details of asking this question, so that you can truly shift a blame-focused discussion into problem solving. As this book draws to a close, I'd like to again lay out the simple three-step approach to making proposals:

Step 1: Make a proposal that contains **Who** does **What, Where**, and **When.**
Step 2: Ask and answer questions about the proposal.
Step 3: Respond with "Yes," "No," or "I'll think about it."

This approach helps manage and solve problems with high-conflict people in several ways:
- It shows that there's more than one "right" answer.
- It shows that you can't be wrong when making a proposal.
- It separates the person from the problem (from the book *Getting to Yes*).
- It separates the person from the solution (outcome could be yours, mine, or ours).
- It distracts from defensive reacting—it engages a different part of the brain.

In addition to teaching you how to shift a high-conflict person from blaming to problem solving, I have provided many tips for the actual problem-solving or negotiation process. These tips can be used with anyone, even though they were designed for dealing with HCPs. The key principle is shifting them away from blaming and *all-or-nothing thinking* to *flexible thinking*, which is where problems usually get solved.

There are many words you can use to communicate the ideas behind "So, what's your proposal?" You can suggest that the person makes lists, generates options, states preferences, looks at alternatives, and so forth. The main idea is that we engage our problem-solving brains by doing this type of "thinking." When we are engaged in "defensive reacting," on the other hand, it's hard to "think" because reactions tend toward fight, flight, or freeze responses.

Remember, You Can Influence Others

Interestingly, you can influence those around you by whether you attempt to engage their defensive reacting, such as by choosing to criticize them, or whether you try to engage their flexible thinking, such as by asking them, "So, what's your proposal?" It seems that we can direct the attention of other people's brains with our own behavior and responses. And, of course, you can also patiently ask *yourself* this question if you get stuck while trying to solve a problem.

I encourage you to try this method and ask this question often. It does take practice, but I think you'll find that it makes your life easier when dealing with HCPs—or, really, when negotiating with anyone.

At least that's my proposal. What's yours?

Best wishes,
Bill Eddy

References

CHAPTER TWO
The (Brain) Power of this Question

Brain research shows: The information about the differences of the right and left hemispheres of the brain has been drawn from several books, including:

Doidge, N. (2007). *The Brain that Changes Itself: Stories of Personal Triumph from the Frontiers.* New York, NY: Penguin Books.

Goldberg, E. (2005). *The Wisdom Paradox: How Your Mind Can Grow Stronger As Your Brain Grows Older.* New York, NY: Gotham Books.

Schore, A. N. (2003). *Affect Regulation and the Repair of the Self.* New York, NY: W. W. Norton & Company.

Seigel, D. J. (1999). *The Developing Mind: How Relationships and the Brain Interact to Shape Who We Are.* New York, NY: The Guilford Press.

Seigel, D. J. (2007). *The Mindful Brain: Reflection and Attunement in the Cultivation of Well-Being.* New York, NY: W. W. Norton & Company.

Mirror neurons: Iacoboni, M. (2008). *Mirroring People: The New Science of How We Connect with Others.* New York, NY: Farrar, Straus and Giroux.

Corpus callosum: Teicher, M. H. (2002). Scars That Won't Heal: The Neurobiology of Child Abuse. *Scientific American,* 286 (3), 68-75.

Neurons that fire together, wire together: Doidge, N. (2007). *The Brain that Changes Itself: Stories of Personal Triumph from the Frontiers.* New York, NY: Penguin Books, p. 64.

For more on HCPs: Eddy, B. (2008). *It's All Your Fault! 12 Tips for Managing People Who Blame Others for Everything*. Scottsdale, AZ: High Conflict Institute Press.

CHAPTER THREE
Making Proposals with Three Simple Steps

... "positions" make it harder to negotiate: Fisher, R. and Ury, W. (1981). *Getting to Yes: Negotiating Agreement Without Giving In*. New York, NY: Penguin Books.

CHAPTER FOUR
Dealing with Resistance

The classic book on this subject: Fisher, R. and Ury, W. (1981). *Getting to Yes: Negotiating Agreement Without Giving In*. New York, NY: Penguin Books.

CHAPTER FIVE
Brainstorming at Work

Brainstorming Alone versus in Groups: Cain, S. (2012, 2013). *Quiet: The Power of Introverts in a World That Can't Stop Talking*. New York, NY: Broadway Books. "...some forty years of research has reached the same startling conclusion.... performance gets worse as group size increases" p. 88.

CHAPTER SIX
Choices in Education

The anxiety level of today's children: Twenge, J. M. and Campbell, W. K. (2009). *The Narcissism Epidemic: Living in the Age of Entitlement*. New York, NY: Free Press.

CHAPTER EIGHT
Realistic Options in Communities

The Dogs: Zennie, M. and Collman, A. (Oct. 28, 2013). US pharmacist shot dead four of his neighbors and their dogs because animals 'were barking too loud'. *Daily Mail* (United Kingdom).

http://www.dailymail.co.uk/news/article-2478716/Michael-Guzzo-shot-dead-4-neighbors-dogs-animals-barking.html

The Party: Jones, J. H. Neighbors' feud behind shootings: Poway gunman had been charged with assault in '08. San Diego Union-Tribune. http://web.utsandiego.com/news/2010/Apr/05/poway-shootings-rooted-longtime-fued-between-neigh/

CHAPTER TEN
Participating in Politics
In terms of getting work done in Congress: Willis, D. (May 28, 2014). A Do-Nothing Congress? Well, Pretty Close. *The New York Times.*

Why is this happening? Kiefer, F. (April 14, 2014). Playing to their crowds. *The Christian Science Monitor Weekly.*

The City Council: Garrick, D. (May 1, 2014). Council Could Decide Wage. *U-T San Diego.* The book example uses facts contained in this newspaper article, but the dialog is entirely fabricated. There is no indication that any real person involved is an HCP.

The "Third Rail" of Politics: Kull, S. (March 10, 2014). How the American people would fix Social Security. *The Christian Science Monitor Weekly.* The book example uses facts contained in this magazine article, but the dialog is entirely fabricated. There is no indication that any real person involved is an HCP.

About the Author

William A. ("Bill") Eddy is President of High Conflict Institute based in San Diego, California. He is a Certified Family Law Specialist in California with over 20 years' experience representing clients in family court and providing divorce mediation out of court. Prior to becoming a lawyer, he worked as a Licensed Clinical Social Worker with 12 years' experience providing therapy to children, adults, couples, and families in psychiatric hospitals and outpatient clinics.

As President and Co-founder of High Conflict Institute, Bill has become an international speaker on the subject of high-conflict personalities to attorneys, judges, mediators, therapists, human resource, EAP, and collaborative professionals, in over 25 states, Canada, France, Sweden, Australia, and New Zealand. High Conflict Institute is dedicated to providing training, resources, and program development to professionals dealing with high-conflict personalities in legal disputes, workplace disputes, health care disputes, and education disputes. The New Ways for Families™ program was developed by Bill in 2009 for the High Conflict Institute as an intervention method for potentially high-conflict families in family courts. His New Ways for Mediation™ method was developed in 2013 to provide more structure and skills for potentially high-conflict clients of any type of mediation.

He is on the faculty of the National Judicial College, providing training to state and federal judges in handling high-conflict people in court, and is also a part-time faculty member of the Strauss Institute for Dispute Resolution at the School of Law at

Pepperdine University. He serves as the Senior Family Mediator at the National Conflict Resolution Center in San Diego, California, and has taught Negotiation and Mediation for six years at the University of San Diego School of Law.

Bill obtained his law degree in 1992 from the University of San Diego, a Master of Social Work degree in 1981 from San Diego State University, and a bachelor's degree in Psychology in 1970 from Case Western Reserve University. He began his career as a youth social worker in a changing neighborhood in New York City. He considers conflict resolution the theme of his varied career.

If you would like to send an email about your experiences, what you've learned from this book, or anything else, please contact Bill at info@highconflictinstitute.com or (619) 221-9108. You can read Bill's blog at www.highconflictinstitute.com and click on "Blog" in the menu bar.

Printed in the USA
CPSIA information can be obtained
at www.ICGtesting.com
JSHW011036020424
60411JS00011B/21